Angkor Wat

Andrew Spooner

Credits

Footprint credits
Editor: Alan Murphy
Production and Layout: Patrick Dawson, Elysia Alim, Danielle Bricker
Maps: Kevin Feeney

Managing Director: Andy Riddle
Commercial Director: Patrick Dawson
Publisher: Alan Murphy
Publishing Managers: Felicity Laughton, Nicola Gibbs
Digital Editors: Jo Williams, Tom Mellors
Marketing and PR: Liz Harper
Sales: Diane McEntee
Advertising: Renu Sibal
Finance and Administration: Elizabeth Taylor

Photography credits
Front cover: Angkor Wat temple, Luciano Mortula/Shutterstock
Back cover: bbbar/Shutterstock

Printed in Great Britain by CPI Antony Rowe, Chippenham, Wiltshire

MIX
Paper from responsible sources
FSC
www.fsc.org
FSC® C013604

Every effort has been made to ensure that the facts in this guidebook are accurate. However, travellers should still obtain advice from consulates, airlines, etc about travel and visa requirements before travelling. The authors and publishers cannot accept responsibility for any loss, injury or inconvenience however caused.

Publishing information
Footprint *Focus Angkor Wat*
1st edition
© Footprint Handbooks Ltd
August 2011

ISBN: 978 1 908206 14 5
CIP DATA: A catalogue record for this book is available from the British Library

® Footprint Handbooks and the Footprint mark are a registered trademark of Footprint Handbooks Ltd

Published by Footprint
6 Riverside Court
Lower Bristol Road
Bath BA2 3DZ, UK
T +44 (0)1225 469141
F +44 (0)1225 469461
footprinttravelguides.com

Distributed in the USA by Globe Pequot Press, Guilford, Connecticut

The content of Footprint *Focus Angkor Wat* has been taken directly from Footprint's *Cambodia Handbook* which was researched and written by Andrew Spooner.

Contents

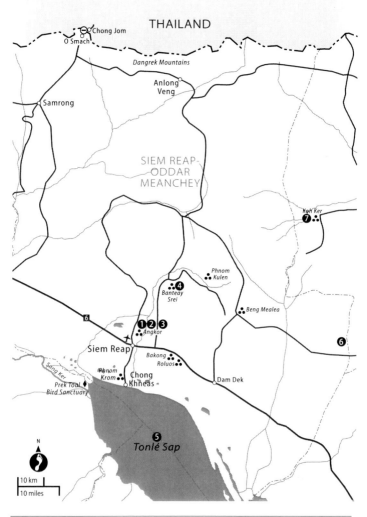

THAILAND

Chong Jom
O Smach
Dangrek Mountains
Anlong Veng
Samrong
SIEM REAP-
ODDAR
MEANCHEY
Koh Ker **7**
Phnom
Kulen
4
Banteay
Srei
Beng Mealea
1 **2** **3**
Angkor
6
Siem Reap
Bakong
Roluos
6
Phnom
Krom
Chong
Khneas
Dam Dek
Song Ker
Prek Toal
Bird Sanctuary
5
Tonlé Sap

N

10 km
10 miles

An enormous and elaborately detailed complex, the ancient temple city of Angkor Wat has remained the heart and soul of Cambodia for almost two millennia. And, despite its popularity with ever-growing throngs of visitors, this is still a historical site that exceeds expectation. Included in the gargantuan complex lie legions of magical temples which attest to the ability of bygone artisans, from the intricate Banteay Srei, with its detailed carvings to the beaming faces of the Bayon. Visitors also flock to jungle-clad Ta Prohm, where tentacle-like foliage entwined around the temple provides an insight into how earlier explorers would have discovered it.

The town of Siem Reap has graduated from Angkor's service centre to an international tourist hub, teeming with modern restaurants and upmarket hotels. Fortunately, the settlement still retains much of its original charm, with old colonial shopfronts, misty lamp-lit streets and a bustling market area. A short trip from Siem Reap is the Tonlé Sap, Southeast Asia's largest freshwater lake, scattered with many floating villages.

North of Siem Reap is Anlong Veng, the hauntingly beautiful former stronghold of the Khmer Rouge. Although short on tourist sites, the town will be of interest to history buffs.

If you travel by road from Angkor to Phnom Penh you'll pass through Kompong Thom and Cambodia's central region. This is certainly a place for the more independent-minded traveller who will put up with tough roads and sparse public transportation in order to be rewarded with amazing temples, beautiful jungle scenery and some of the friendliest small villages in the country.

Planning your trip

When to go and what to see

Angkor and the central region's busiest period coincides with the dry season, November to February. Not only is this the driest time of year it is also the coolest (although it can still be unbearably hot). Be advised that this time of year is also incredibly busy and you may find yourself experiencing the drama of Angkor along with hundreds of Korean and Chinese tour groups. The monsoon lasts from June to October/November. It can be incredibly wet and muddy at this time of year but you may find you have an entire temple to yourself.

Tourist information

There is a new tourist office open at the far end of Sivatha Street (towards the crocodile farm), open in the morning between 0730-1100 and in the afternoon 1430-1700. **Khmer Angkor Tour Guide Association** is in the same building and open every day. See below.

Guides can be invaluable when navigating the temples, with the majority being able to answer most questions about Angkor as well as providing additional information about Cambodian culture and history. Most hotels and travel agents will be able to point you in the direction of a good guide. The **Khmer Angkor Tour Guide Association** ① *T063-964347, www.khmerangkortourguide.com*, has well-trained guides. Most of the guides here are very well briefed and some speak English better than others. The going rate is US$20-25 per day.

Angkor Conservation is a specialist research institution, just off the main road to Angkor and about 1 km from the Grand Hotel (signed Conservation d'Angkor). Many statues, stelae and linga found at Angkor are stored here to prevent theft. It is accessible by special appointment only. Contact the Ministry of Culture in Phnom Penh for a written invitation which needs to describe the research objectives of the visitor.

Temple fees and opening hours A one-day pass costs US$20, three-day pass US$40, seven-day pass US$60. The seven day pass is valid for any seven days (doesn't have to be consecutive) one month from the purchase date. Most people will be able to cover the majority of the temples within three days. If you buy your ticket after 1715 the day beforehand, you get a free sunset thrown in. The complex is open daily 0530-1830. You will need to pay additional fees if you wish to visit Beng Melea (US$5), Phnom Kulen (US$20) or Koh Ker (US$10) - payable at the individual sites.

Safety Landmines were planted on some outlying paths to prevent Khmer Rouge guerrillas from infiltrating the temples; they have pretty much all been cleared by now, but it is safer to stick to well-used paths. Wandering anywhere in the main temple complexes is perfectly safe. Be wary of snakes in the dry season. The very poisonous Hanuman snake (lurid green) is fairly common in the area.

Photography Don't forget to ask the permission of the people who you wish to include in your shots. In general, the best time to photograph most temples is before 0900 and after 1630.

Don't miss ...

Itineraries

The temples are scattered over an area in excess of 160 sq km. There are three so-called 'circuits'. The **Petit Circuit** (17 km) takes in the main central temples including Angkor Wat, Bayon, Baphuon and the Terrace of the Elephants. The **Grand Circuit** (26 km) takes a wider route, including smaller temples like Ta Prohm, East Mebon, Pre Rup and Neak Pean. The **Roluos Group Circuit** ventures further afield still, taking in the temples near Roluos: Lolei, Preah Ko and Bakong.

The order of visiting is a matter of opinion; here are some options:
Half day South Gate of Angkor Thom, Bayon, Angkor Wat.

One day Angkor Wat (sunrise or sunset), South Gate of Angkor Thom, Angkor Thom (Bayon, Terrace of the Elephants, Royal Palace) and Ta Prohm. This is a hefty schedule for one day; you'll need to arrive after 1615 and finish just after 1700 the following day.

Two days The same as above but with the inclusion of the rest of the Angkor Thom, Preah Srah Srang (sunrise) and at a push, Banteay Srei.

Three days – Day 1 Sunrise at Angkor Wat; morning South Gate of Angkor Thom, Angkor complex (aside from Bayon); Ta Prohm; late afternoon-sunset at Bayon. **Day 2** Srah Srang; morning Banteay Kdei and Banteay Srei; late afternoon Preah Khan; at Angkor Wat. **Day 3** Sunrise and morning Roluos; afternoon Ta Keo and sunset either Bakheng or Angkor Wat.

Those choosing to stay one or two days longer should try to work Banteay Samre, East Mebon, Neak Pean and Thomannon into their itinerary. A further two to three days warrants a trip to Prasat Kravan, Ta Som, Beng Melea and Kbal Spean.

Getting there

Air

International connections with Cambodia are still poor – but improving – and most travellers will need to route themselves through Kuala Lumpur, Singapore or Bangkok, all of which have good onward connections to both Phnom Penh and Siem Reap. There are direct flights only from within the region.

To/from Phnom Penh These airlines currently operate international services to Phnom Penh's Pochentong Airport: **Air Asia** – Kuala Lumpur, Bangkok; **Bangkok Airways** – Bangkok; **China Airlines** – Taipei; **Silk Air** – Singapore; **Dragon Air** – Hong Kong; **Thai** – Bangkok; **Malaysia Airlines** – Kuala Lumpur; **Vietnam Airlines** – Vientiane, Ho Chi Minh City; **Shanghai Air** – Shanghai; **China Southern** – Guangzhou; **Eva** – Taipei; **Jet Star** – Singapore; **Korean & Asiana** – Incheon. New Cambodian national flag carrier **Cambodia Angkor Air** flies to and from Ho Chi Minh City. See Phnom Penh transport, page , for contact details for each airline.

To/from Siem Reap There are connections with **Bangkok Airways** – Bangkok; **Air Asia** – Kuala Lumpur; **Malaysia** – Kuala Lumpur; **Vietnam** – Hanoi and Ho Chi Minh City; **Jet Star** – Singapore; **Silk** – Singapore; **Korean & Asiana** – Incheon; **Lao Aviation** – Vientiane.

Getting to Singapore, Kuala Lumpur and Bangkok Travelling to any one of these three main hubs by air offers up some of the cheapest and best connected flying on the planet. Due to high tourist and business demand pretty much every major airline from every major country in the world flies here. From these three different places a range of budget and short-haul carriers can then link the traveller to Cambodia. Direct flight times into each of these hubs are roughly 12 hours from Europe, 16 hours from the west coast of the USA and eight to 12 hours from Australia and New Zealand.

Singapore Some 20 km from downtown Singapore, **Changi Airport**, www.changi.airport.com.sg, is Southeast Asia's busiest airport with most major long-haul airlines flying here from throughout the world and almost every major city in the region connected to it by air. This airport has incredible facilities including hotels, cinemas, spas, dozens of places to eat, great shopping, lots of comfortable seating and free Wi-Fi, making it easily the best place in the region to wait in between flights. **Singapore Airlines**, www.singaporeair.com – often voted one of the best in the world – is the national carrier. Another important Singaporean airline is SilkAir, www.silkair.com, which flies to numerous short- and mid-range destinations. Changi is also a hub for budget Asian airlines. There is a separate budget terminal – imaginatively named the **Budget Terminal**, www.btsingapore.com. A free shuttle bus service links it with Terminal 2.

Bangkok Bangkok's **Suvarnabhumi International Airport**, one of the biggest airports in the world, has extensive connections to major cities in Europe, New Zealand and Australia. The USA is less well served, though it is possible to connect to US-bound flights via Taiwan, Japan and Korea. **Thai Airways**, www.thaiairways.com, is the national carrier.

While arriving at Suvarnabhumi is relatively painless, passenger facilities at the airport are poor. In 2007, due to a mixture of runway cracks and lack of working facilities, the old airport, **Don Muang**, 25 km to the north of the city, was forced to re-open for some domestic routes.

Despite the problems, Bangkok is still an excellent hub to reach much of the rest of the region. **Thai Airways** routing is extensive with flights to most major and capital cities in the region. Bangkok is also one of the primary hubs for budget and short-haul carriers. The main players are **Air Asia**, www.airasia.com, **Jetstar**, www.jetstar.com, and **Bangkok Airways**, www.bangkokair.com.

Chiang Mai in the north and Phuket in the south also have international airports with some scheduled short-haul connections, mainly with **Air Asia** and **Thai Airways**.

Kuala Lumpur The Malaysian capital's **Kuala Lumpur International Airport (KLIA)** is now positioning itself as a major regional hub with the national carrier, **Malaysian Airlines**, among others, providing long-haul flights from Europe, Australia/New Zealand and the USA and short-haul flights throughout the region. The KLIA airport itself is well run, efficient and comfortable.

For budget travellers there's the nearby **KLIA Low Cost Carrier Terminal (LCCT)**, 20 minutes by shuttle bus from the main terminal. It offers some of the most extensive budget airline routings in the region, primarily with **Air Asia**, www.airasia.com, which is even now offering budget long-haul flights to the UK and Australia as well as all regional capitals and many other major destinations. Travellers should be aware that the LCCT has the most basic facilities, with long queues and bad service – transiting here can be an ordeal.

Airport departure tax International departure from Cambodia is US$25 for international flights. There is a US$6 departure tax on internal flights.

Road
It is possible to enter Cambodia, overland, from Thailand, Vietnam and Laos. Travellers coming from Thailand usually cross at **Poipet** - the road from here to Siem Reap is now massively improved cutting journey times to two hours. There are other overland entries from Thailand through Pailin (very rough roads), Anlong Veng (reasonably rough roads) and Koh Kong. As ever, the overland route from Vietnam via **Moc Bai** is the slow but cheap option for travellers coming from the east, and the border crossing at **Omsano** has enabled those coming from Vietnam to take the more scenic river route via Chau Doc. There is a brand new scenic border open via Kep between Cambodia and Vietnam (Ha Tien). There is also a crossing between Phnom Penh and Tinh Bien in Vietnam. The border crossing from Laos, close to the town at **Stung Treng**, is open but no visas are issued at the border with Laos.

Sea/river
There are sailings from **Ho Chi Minh City** (Saigon) to Phnom Penh. Ho Chi Minh City tour cafés run minibuses to **Chau Doc** and on to the border which is crossed on foot. Change to a speed boat which will take you to **Neak Luong** in Cambodia. Disembark here and take a taxi/pickup along Route 1 to Phnom Penh.

Some boats travel from Thailand's Koh Chang/Trat area to Hat Lek for the Koh Kong border crossing but these are mostly seasonal and vary according to demand.
Cruise ships visit the international seaport of Sihanoukville.

Getting around

Angkor is served by the airport at Siem Reap, 7 km from town. Boats also travel from Phnom Penh and Battambang. Buses and shared taxis also ply the route from the capital.
▸ See Transport, page 73.

Most of the temples within the Angkor complex (except the Roluos Group) are in an area extending across a 25 km radius roughly 8 km north of Siem Reap. The Roluos Group are 13 km east of Siem Reap and Banteay Srei 32 km. Cars with drivers and guides are available from larger hotels for US$25-30 per day plus US$25 for a guide. An excellent guiding service by car is provided by Mr Hak, T012-540336, www.angkortaxidriver.com, who offers a variety of packages and tours around Angkor and the surrounding area. Expect to pay US$10-12 per day for a moto unless the driver speaks good English in which case the price will be higher. This price will cover trips to the Roluos Group but not to Banteay Srei. There is no need to add more than a dollar or two to the price for getting to Banteay Srei unless the driver is also a guide and can demonstrate to you that he is genuinely going to show you around.

Tuk-tuks (remourk in Khmer) and their ilk have appeared on the scene in recent years and are quite a popular option for two people, US$14-17 a day (maximum of two people). **Bicycle hire** costs US$2-3 per day from most guesthouses and is a good option for those who feel reasonably familiar with the area as the roads are pretty good. The White Bicycles scheme, set up by Norwegian ex-pats (see Transport, page 74), offers bikes for US$2 per day with US$1.50 of that going straight into local charities and no commission to the hotels and is recommended. If you are on a limited schedule and only have a day or two at the temples you won't be able to cover an awful lot of them on a pedal bike as the searing temperatures and sprawling layout can limit even the most advanced cyclists. Angkor Wat and Banteay Srei have official parking sites, 1000 riel (US$0.25), and at the other temples you can quite safely park and lock your bikes in front of a drink stall.

For those wishing to see Angkor from a different perspective it is possible to charter a **helicopter**. In many ways, it is only from the air that you can really grasp the size and scale of Angkor and a short flight will certainly be a memorable experience. Try **Helicopters Cambodia**, T063-963316, www.helicopterscambodia.com, who offer flights from US$75 per person. **Elephants** are stationed near the Bayon or at the South Gate of Angkor Thom during the day. In the evenings, they can be found at the bottom of Phnom Bakheng, taking tourists up to the summit for sunset.

The Angkor site can be a real struggle for **disabled or frail persons**, the stairs are 90 degrees steep and semi-restoration of areas means visitors will sometimes need to climb over piles of bricks. Still, many people manage to do it. Hiring an aide to help you climb stairs, etc, is a very good idea and costs around US$5-10 a day.

Kompong Thom provides a convenient stop-off point halfway between Siem Reap and Phnom Penh on the continually improving National Highway 6 and all buses travelling between the two destinations will stop in Kompong Thom. The rest of the central region contains some of the country's worst roads making the area a little tricky to navigate. Public transport is limited and in some of the more remote areas it is almost non-existent. In larger towns, like Kompong Thom, there are a range of options from shared taxi to buses but in other spots you might find yourself hopping in the back of someone's tractor. To access sites like Preah Khan or Koh Ker a larger dirt bike or 4WD is the best option. Most roads are constructed from dirt, so travelling to the temples or smaller towns becomes very difficult, or near impossible, in the wet season. The region is still littered with mines, many of which aren't marked, so stay on clearly marked tracks.

Sleeping and eating price codes

Sleeping

$$$$ over US$100   **$$$**   US$46-99

$$ US$21-45   **$**   Under US$20

Prices are for a double room in high season, including taxes.

Eating

¶¶¶   Expensive over US$12   ¶¶   Mid-range US$6-12

¶   Cheap under US$6

Prices refer to the cost of a two-course meal for one person, excluding drinks or tips.

Sleeping and eating

Accommodation standards in Cambodia have greatly improved over the last couple of years. Phnom Penh now has a good network of genuine boutique hotels – arguably they are overpriced and sometimes management can be a bit Fawlty Towers but the bar has certainly been raised. Siem Reap, without doubt, has now become a destination for the upmarket international traveller. The range, depth and quality of accommodation here is of an excellent standard and is on a par with anywhere else in Asia. Even if you travel to some of the smaller, less visited towns, family-run Chinese-style hotels should now provide hot water, air conditioning and cable TV even if they can't provide first-class service. These places are often the best bargains in the country as many of the cheap backpacker places, while very, very cheap, are mostly hovels.

More expensive hotels have safety boxes in the rooms. In cheaper hotels it is not uncommon for things to be stolen from bedrooms. In Phnom Penh this poses a real dilemma for it is more dangerous to take valuables on to the night time streets. Most hotels and guesthouses will accept valuables for safekeeping but do keep a close eye on your cash.

Eating

For a country that has suffered and starved in the way Cambodia has, eating for fun as opposed to for survival, has yet to catch on as a pastime. There are some good restaurants and things are improving but don't expect Cambodia to be a smaller version of Thailand, or its cuisine even to live up to the standards of Laos. Cambodian food shows clear links with the cuisines of neighbouring countries: Thailand, Vietnam, and to a lesser extent, Laos. The influence of the French colonial period is also in evidence, most clearly in the availability of good French bread. Chinese food is also available owing to strong business ties between Cambodia and China. True Khmer food is difficult to find and much that the Khmers would like to claim as indigenous food is actually of Thai, French or Vietnamese origin. Curries, soups, rice and noodle-based dishes, salads, fried vegetables and sliced meats all feature in Khmer cooking.

Phnom Penh and Siem Reap have the best **restaurants** with French, Japanese, Italian and Indian food being available. But those who want to sample a range of dishes and get a feel for Khmer cuisine should head for the nearest market where dishes will be cooked on order in a wok – known locally as a *chhnang khteak*.

Fishy business

Every national cuisine has its signature dish and in Cambodia it is **prahok**, a strong, pungent, fermented fish paste that's been used to flavour Khmer dishes for centuries.

Cambodians swear by it and use it in everything from dips and soups, through to a simple accompaniment for rice. Reports suggest that 95% of Cambodians eat the delicacy, so it is no surprise that the practice of making it has passed down from generation to generation.

The Fisheries Department believe that in some areas 10% of fish caught are set aside for the manufacture of *prahok*. The paste is made by stomping on hundreds of small fish and fish heads in a large bucket. Once the fish is transformed into a thick brown paste it's left in the sun for a day to ferment. Salt is then added and the paste is put in jars and sold.

Locals suggest that *prahok* can be eaten after a month of maturation, but most consider the paste to be at its best after a few years. This is a Cambodian delicacy, like sushi or parmesan cheese. It may taste a bit unusual at first and is something of an acquired taste (if you get past the smell).

International **soft drinks** are widely available in Cambodia. If there is a national drink in Cambodia, then it has to be **tea** which is drunk without sugar or milk. **Coffee** is also available black or 'crème' with sweetened condensed milk. That ubiquitous and well-known brand of cola is available as well as most other international soft drinks. Soda water with lemon, *soda kroch chhmar*, is a popular drink. **Bottled water** is widely available; local mineral water too. **Fruit smoothies** – known locally as *tikalok* – are found at stalls with that give-away food processor on the counter. If you want to avoid consuming your fruit with horrendous quantities of sugar then make sure you make your intentions clear. Most market stands will serve great fruit smoothies, but again, you might wish to request minimal sweet milk and stipulate whether you want egg or not. Fresh **milk** is hard to find outside of metropolitan areas.

Local and imported **beers** are available. Of the locally brewed beers the three most common are Angkor Beer, Anchor and ABC Stout – available on draught, in bottles and cans. VB or Victoria Bitter is also brewed locally but is much less common. Beer Lao, although imported, is usually the cheapest and also one of the best.

Responsible travel

Since the early 1990s there has been a phenomenal growth in 'ecotourism', which promotes and supports the conservation of natural environments and is also fair and equitable to local communities. While the authenticity of some ecotourism operators needs to be interpreted with care, there is clearly both a huge demand for this type of activity and also significant opportunities to support worthwhile conservation and social development initiatives by this means. **Green Globe** (T020-7730 4428, www.greenglobe21.com) and **Responsible Travel** (www.responsibletravel.com) offer advice for travellers on selecting destinations and sites focused on conservation and sustainable development.

How big is your footprint?

The benefits of international travel are self-evident for both hosts and travellers: employment, increased understanding of different cultures, business and leisure opportunities. At the same time there is clearly a downside to the industry. Where visitor pressure is high or poorly regulated, adverse impacts to society and the natural environment may occur. In order to ensure your contribution to the host nation is a positive one, **Tourism Concern** has these guidelines on its website, www.tourismconcern.org.uk.

→ Learn about the country you're visiting. Start enjoying your travels before you leave by tapping into as many sources of information as you can.

→ Think about where your money goes – be fair and realistic about how cheaply you travel. Try and put money into local people's hands; drink local beer or fruit juice rather than imported brands, and stay in locally-owned accommodation.

→ Open your mind to new cultures and traditions. It can transform your holiday experience and you'll earn respect and be more readily welcomed by local people.

→ Think about what happens to your rubbish: take biodegradable products and a water filter bottle. Be sensitive to limited resources like water, fuel and electricity.

→ Help preserve local wildlife and habitats by respecting rules and regulations, such as sticking to footpaths, not standing on coral and not buying products made from endangered plants or animals.

→ Use your guidebook as a starting point, not the only source of information. Talk to local people, then discover your own adventure.

In addition, the **International Eco-Tourism Society** (www.ecotourism.org), **Tourism Concern** (T020-7753 3330, www.tourismconcern.org.uk), and **Planeta** (www.planeta.com), develop and promote ecotourism projects in destinations all over the world and their websites provide details for initiatives throughout Southeast Asia.

For opportunities to participate directly in scientific research and development projects, contact **Earthwatch** (www.earthwatch.org), **Discovery International** (www.discovery initiatives.com) and the **Nautilus Institute** (www.nautilus.org), which focuses on environmental and sustainability issues in the Asia-Pacific region.

Local customs and conduct

Cambodians are relaxed, easy-going people who are unlikely to take or give offence. Decent behaviour is never going to upset the Cambodians and it is difficult for normal people to offend them unwittingly. Only crass behaviour, such as patting people on the head or invading their homes uninvited, will upset them. One of the sheer joys of Cambodia and the reason for its enduring popularity among travellers is the simplicity of the way of life and the population's tolerance of others.

Temples When visiting a temple do dress respectfully (keep bare flesh to a minimum) and take off your hat and shoes. Put your legs to one side and try not to point the soles of your feet at anyone or the Buddha image. Females are not to touch monks or sit beside them on public transport. Remove shoes before entering temples and a small donation is often appropriate.

Greeting Cambodians use their traditional greeting – the 'wai' – bowing with their hands held together. As a foreigner, shaking hands is perfectly acceptable.

In private homes It is polite to take your shoes off on entering the house and a small present goes down well if you are invited for a meal.

General Displays of anger or exasperation are considered unacceptable and therefore reflect very badly on the individual. Accordingly, even in adversity, Khmers (like the Thais) will keep smiling. Displays of affection are also considered embarrassing and should be avoided in public areas. Try not to pat anyone on the head. To beckon someone, use your hand with the palm facing downwards. Pointing is rude.

Women should **dress appropriately**. Short skirts, midriff-baring and cleavage-exposing tops and tight outfits are deemed clothes that prostitutes wear. If you choose to dress like this then you may unwittingly attract undesirable attention and potentially offend some people.

Essentials A-Z

Accident and emergency

Contact the relevant emergency service and your embassy. Obtain police/medical reports in order to file insurance claims.

Emergency services Police: 117, Fire: 118, Ambulance: 119.

Electricity

Voltage 220. Sockets are usually round 2-pin.

Embassies and consulates.

A full list of Cambodian embassies and consulates can be found on www.cambodia.gov.kh.

Australia and New Zealand 5 Canterbury Cres, Deakin, Canberra, ACT 2600, T+61-2-6273 1259, www.embassyof cambodia.org.nz/au.htm.

France 4 rue Adolphe Yvon, 75116 Paris, T+33-1-4503 4720, ambcambodgeparis@ mangoosta.fr.

Germany Benjamin-Vogelsdorf Strasse, 213187, Berlin, T+49-30-4863 7901, www.kambodscha-botschaft.de.

Japan 8-6-9, Akasaka, Minato-Ku, Tokyo 1070052, T+81-3-5412 8522, www.cambodianembassy.jp.

Laos Thadeua Rd, KM2 Vientiane, BP34, T+856-2-131 4950, recamlao@laotel.com.

Thailand 185 Rajdamri Rd, Lumpini Patumwan, Bangkok 10330, T+66-2-254 6630, recbkk@cscoms.com.

United Kingdom and **Scandinavian countries**, 64 Brondesbury Park, Willesden Green, London, NW6 7AT, T020-8451 7850, www.cambodianembassy.org.uk.

USA 4500, 16th St, NW Washington, DC20011, T+1-202-726 8042, www.embassy.org/cambodia.

Vietnam 71 Tran Hung Dao St, Hanoi, T844-942 4789, arch@fpt.vn; 41 Phung Khac Khoan, Ho Chi Minh City, T848-829 2751, cambocg@hcm.vmn.vn.

Health

See your GP or travel clinic at least 6 weeks before departure for general advice on travel risks and vaccinations. Try phoning a specialist travel clinic if your own doctor is unfamiliar with health conditions in Cambodia. Make sure you have sufficient medical travel insurance, get a dental check, know your own blood group and if you suffer a long-term condition such as diabetes or epilepsy, obtain a **Medic Alert** bracelet/necklace (www.medicalert.co.uk). If you wear glasses, take a copy of your prescription.

Vaccinations

It is advisable to vaccinate against polio, tetanus, typhoid, hepatitis A, and rabies if going to more remote areas. Yellow fever does not exist in Cambodia, but the authorities may wish to see a certificate if you have recently arrived from an endemic area in Africa or South America. Japanese Encephalitis may be advised for some areas, depending on the duration of the trip and proximity to rice-growing and pig-farming areas.

Health risks

The most common cause of travellers' **diarrhoea** is from eating food contaminated food. Swimming in sea or river water that has been contaminated by sewage can also be a cause; ask locally if it is safe. Diarrhoea may be also caused by viruses, bacteria (such as E-coli), protozoal (such as giardia), salmonella and cholera. It may be accompanied by vomiting or by severe abdominal pain. Any kind of diarrhoea responds well to the replacement of water and salts. Sachets of rehydration salts can be bought in most chemists and can be dissolved in boiled water. If the symptoms persist, consult a doctor. Tap water in the major cities is in theory safe to drink but it may be advisable to err on the side of caution and drink only bottled or boiled water. Avoid having ice in drinks unless you trust that it is from a reliable source.

Mosquitoes are more of a nuisance than a serious hazard but some, of course, are carriers of serious diseases such as **malaria**, which exists in most of Cambodia except Phnom Penh. The choice of malaria prophylaxis will need to be something other than chloroquine for most people, since there is such a high level of resistance to it. Always check with your doctor or travel clinic for the most up-to-date advice on the best anti-malarials to use. It's also sensible to avoid being bitten as much as possible. Sleep off the ground and use a mosquito net and some kind of insecticide. Mosquito coils release insecticide as they burn and are available in many shops, as are tablets of insecticide, which are placed on a heated mat plugged into a wall socket.

Each year there is the possibility that **avian flu** or **SARS** might rear their ugly heads. Check the news reports. If there is a problem in an area you are due to visit you may be advised to have an ordinary flu shot or to seek expert advice.

There are high rates of HIV in the region, especially among sex workers.

If you get sick

Contact your embassy or consulate for a list of doctors and dentists who speak your language, or at least some English. Doctors and health facilities in major cities are also listed in the Directory sections of this book. Make sure you have adequate insurance (see below). Hospitals are not recommended anywhere in Cambodia (even at some of the clinics that profess to be 'international'). If you fall ill or are injured your best bet is to get yourself quickly to either **Bumrungrad Hospital** or **Bangkok Nursing Home**, both in Bangkok. Both hospitals are of an exceptional standard, even in international terms.

Thailand

Bumrungrad Hospital, Soi 3 Sukhumvit, Bangkok, T+66 2-667 1000, www.bumrungrad. com. The best option: a world-class hospital with brilliant medical facilities.

Useful websites

www.btha.org British Travel Health Association.

www.cdc.gov US government site that gives excellent advice on travel health and details of disease outbreaks.

www.fco.gov.uk British Foreign and Commonwealth Office travel site has useful information on each country, people, climate and a list of UK embassies/consulates.

www.fitfortravel.scot.nhs.uk A-Z of vaccine/health advice for each country.

www.numberonehealth.co.uk Travel screening services, vaccine and travel health advice, email/SMS text vaccine reminders and screens returned travellers for tropical diseases.

Money

The **riel** is the official currency though US dollars are widely accepted and easily exchanged. At the time of going to press the **exchange rates** were US$1 = 4115, UK£1= 6665, €1 = 5911.

In Phnom Penh and other towns most goods and services are priced in dollars and there is little need to buy riel.In remote rural areas prices are quoted in riel (except accommodation). In many places, particularly near the Thai border, Thai baht can often be used as well.

Money can be exchanged in banks and hotels. US dollar traveller's cheques are easiest to exchange – commission ranges from 1% to 3%. Cash advances on credit cards are available. Credit card facilities are limited but some banks, hotels and restaurants do accept them, mostly in the tourist centres. **ANZ Royal Bank** has recently opened a number of ATMs throughout Phnom Penh and Siem Reap. Machines are also now appearing in other towns and a full ATM network should be established in the next couple of years. Most machines give US dollars only.

Opening hours

Shops Daily from 0800-2000. Some, however, stay open for a further hour or 2, especially in tourist centres. Most markets open daily from 0530/0600 and 1700.
Banks Mon-Fri 0800-1600. Some close 1100-1300. Some major branches are open until 1100 on Sat.
Offices Mon-Fri 0730-1130, 1330-1630.
Restaurants, cafés and bars Daily from 0700-0800, although some open earlier. Bars are meant to close at 2400 by law.

Police and the law

A vast array of offences are punishable in Cambodia, from minor traffic violations through to possession of drugs. If you are arrested or are having difficulty with the police contact your embassy immediately. As the police only earn approximately US$20 a month, corruption is a problem and contact should be avoided, unless absolutely necessary. Most services, including the provision of police reports, will require paying bribes. Law enforcement is very haphazard, at times completely subjective and justice can be hard to find. Some smaller crimes can attract large penalties while perpetrators of greater crimes often get off completely.

Safety

Cambodia is not as dangerous as some would have us believe. The country has really moved forward in protecting tourists and violent crimes towards visitors is comparatively low. Since large penalties have been introduced for those who kill or maim tourists, random acts of violence aren't as common these days. Having said that, night time safety on the

streets of Phnom Penh is a problem; robberies and hold-ups are common. Many robbers are armed, so do not resist. As Phnom Penh has a limited taxi service, travel after dark poses a problem. Stick to moto drivers you know. Women are, obviously, particularly targeted by bag snatchers but many bag snatchers will now be chased by the locals, beaten and sometimes even killed. Khmer New Year is known locally as the 'robbery season'. Theft is endemic at this time of year so be on red alert. A common trick around New Year is for robbers to mess around with tourists (usually throwing water and talcum powder in the eyes) and rob them – literally – blind. Leave your valuables in the hotel safe or hidden in your room.

Outside Phnom Penh safety is not as much of a problem. Visitors should be very cautious when walking in the countryside, however, as landmines and other unexploded ordnance is a ubiquitous hazard. Stick to well-worn paths, especially around Siem Reap and when visiting remote temples. Motorbike accidents have serious fatality rates here.

Tipping

Tipping is rare but appreciated. Salaries in restaurants and hotels are low and many staff hope to make up the difference in tips. As with everywhere else, good service should be rewarded.

Visas and immigration

In 2009 Cambodia began an e-visa system which will allow tourists to negotiate arrivals much quicker. The charge is US$20 plus a US$5 admin charge. These visas are valid for 3 months from date of issue for a single entry of 30 days. They can ONLY be used at the following points of entry: Siem Reap Airport, Phnom Penh Airport, Poipet, Koh Kong and Bavet. The usual tourist visas for a 30-day stay are still available on arrival at these and several other entry points. Fill in a form and hand over 1 photograph (4 cm x 6 cm). Tourist visas cost US$20 and your passport must be valid for at least 6 months from the date of entry. More details of the e-visa plus an up-to-date list of border crossings and requirements can be found here http://evisa.mfaic.gov.kh/e-visa/. Cambodia also has missions overseas from which visas can be obtained.

Travellers leaving by land must ensure that their Vietnam visa specifies Moc Bai or Chau Doc as points of entry otherwise they could be turned back. You can apply for a Cambodian visa in Ho Chi Minh City and collect in Hanoi and vice versa.

Extensions can be obtained at the Department for Foreigners on the road to the Airport, T023-581558 (passport photo required). Most travel agents arrange visa extensions for around US$40 for 30 days. Those overstaying their visas are fined US$5 per day, although officials at land crossings often try to squeeze out more.

Weights and measures
Metric.

Angkor and around

Angkor and around

The huge temple complex of Angkor, the ancient capital of the powerful Khmer Empire, is one of the archaeological treasures of Asia and the spiritual and cultural heart of Cambodia. Henri Mouhot, the Frenchman who rediscovered it, wrote that "it is grander than anything of Greece or Rome". Its architectural wonders are, to those that know them, unsurpassed by anything in Europe, Asia or Latin America.

The jungle around Angkor is scattered with many temple complexes which are also covered in this section. The former Khmer Rouge stronghold of Anlong Veng is found north of Siem Reap – the large town that serves the area.

In the central region both Kompong Thom and the less easily accessible T'Beng Meanchey provide hubs to visit the remote archaeological remains of Koh Ker, Sambor Prei Kuk and Preah Khan. You'll also find the more spectacular Preah Vihear in this central region, pressed up tight against a disputed part of the Cambodian-Thai border. Due to recent fighting we recommend visitors heed their home governments' warnings on travel to Preah Vihear and exercise extreme caution.

History

Khmer Empire

Under Jayavarman VII (1181-1218) the Angkor complex stretched more than 25 km east to west and nearly 10 km north to south, approximately the same size as Manhattan. For five centuries (9th-13th) the court of Angkor held sway over a vast territory. At its height, according to a 12th-century Chinese account, Khmer influence spanned half of Southeast Asia, from Burma to the southernmost tip of Indochina and from the borders of Yunnan to the Malay Peninsula. Khmer monuments can be found in the south of Laos and East Thailand as well as in Cambodia. The only threat to this great empire was a riverborne invasion in 1177, when the Cham used a Chinese navigator to pilot their war canoes up the Mekong. Scenes are depicted in bas-reliefs of the Bayon temple.

The kings and construction – the temples and the creators

Jayavarman II (AD 802-835) founded the Angkor Kingdom, then coined Hariharalaya the capital to the north of the Tonlé Sap, in the Roluos Region (Angkor), in AD 802. Later he moved the capital to Phnom Kulen, 40 km northeast of Angkor, where he built a Mountain Temple and Rong Shen shrine. After several years he moved the capital back to the Roluos Region.

Jayavarman III continued his father's legacy and built a number of shrines at Hariharalaya. Many historians believe that he was responsible for the initial construction of the impressive laterite pyramid, Bakong, considered the great precursor to Angkor Wat. Bakong, built to symbolize Mount Meru, was later embellished and developed by Indravarman. Indravarman (AD 877-889) overthrew his predecessor violently and undertook a major renovation campaign in the capital Hariharalaya. The majority of what stands in the Roluos Group today is the work of Indravarman. Among his architectural feats are Preah Ko Temple, built in AD 880, and the remodelling of Bakong (with sandstone cladding). His greatest creation, initiated five days after his coronation, was the 'Sea of Indra', a massive baray (waterbasin), 3.8 km long by 800 m wide. Indravarman is credited with establishing many of the architectural 'norms' for the period that followed. A battle between Indravarman's sons destroyed the palace and the victor and new king Yasovarman I (AD 889-900) moved the capital from Roluos and laid the foundations of Angkor itself. Prior to the move, he constructed Lolei Temple at Roluos on an island in the baray his father built. He dedicated the temple to his ancestors. His new capital at Angkor was called Yasodharapura ('glory-bearing city'), and here he built 100 wooden ashramas (retreats), all of which have disintegrated today. Yasovarman selected Bakheng as the location for his temple-mountain and after flattening the mountain top, set about creating another Mount Meru. The temple he constructed was considered more complex than anything built beforehand – a five-storey pyramid with 108 shrines. A road was then built to link the former and present capitals of Roluos and Bakheng. Like the kings before him, Yasovarman was obliged to construct major waterworks and the construction of the reservoir – the East Baray (now completely dry) – was considered an incredible feat. The baray is eight times larger than his father's 'Sea of Indra' and historian, Claude Jacques, believes it would have taken no less than six million man days to construct. Some also suggest that Yasovarman constructed the temples of Phnom Bok and Phnom Krom.

After Yasovarman's death in AD 900 his son Harshavarman (AD 900-923) assumed power for the next 23 years. During his brief reign, Harshavarman is believed to have built Baksei Chamkrong (northeast of Phnom Bakheng) and Prasat Kravan (the 'Cardamom Sanctuary'). His brother, Ishanarvarman II, resumed power upon his death but no great architectural feats were recorded in this time. In AD 928, Jayavarman IV moved the capital 120 km away to Koh Ker (see page 60). Here he built the grand state temple Prasat Thom, an impressive seven-storey sandstone pyramid. Over the next 20 years as king he

① Angkor, Siem Reap & Roluos

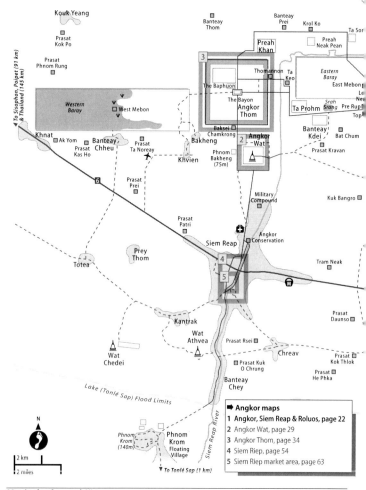

➡ Angkor maps

1 Angkor, Siem Reap & Roluos, page 22
2 Angkor Wat, page 29
3 Angkor Thom, page 34
4 Siem Riep, page 54
5 Siem Riep market area, page 63

undertook the construction of some smaller temples in the Koh Ker area and a baray. Many of the sculptures from his reign are in the National Museum in Phnom Penh.

Following the death of Jayavarman things took a turn for the worse. Chaos ensued under Harshavarman's II (AD 941-944) weak leadership and over the next four years, no monuments were known to be erected. Jayavarman's IV nephew, Rajendravarman, took control of the situation and it's assumed he forcefully relocated the capital back to Angkor. Rather than moving back into the old capital Phnom Bakheng, he marked his own new territory, selecting an area south of the East Baray as his administrative centre. Here, in 1961, he constructed the state temple – Pre Rup and constructed the temple, East Mebon (AD 953), in the middle of the baray. Srah Srang, Kutisvara and Bat Chum were also constructed, with the help of his chief architect, Kavindrarimathana. He also took to task the restoration of Baksei Chamkrong, a temple he held in the highest regard. It was towards the end of his reign that he started construction on Banteay Srei, considered one of the finest examples of Angkorian craftsmanship in the country. Rajendravarman's son became the new king Jayavarman V (AD 968-1001) and he took the royal reigns. The administrative centre was renamed Jayendranagari and yet again, relocated. A new state temple, Ta Keo, was built west of the East Baray. The temple is believed to be somewhat cursed as it was struck by lightening during its construction and never completed. More than compensating for the unfinished Ta Keo was Jayavarman's V continued work on Banteay Srei. Under his supervision the splendid temple was completed and dedicated to his father.

Aside from successfully extending the Khmer Empire's territory King Suryavarman I (1002-1049), made a significant contribution to Khmer architectural heritage. He presided over the creation of a new administrative centre – the Royal Palace (in Angkor Thom) and the huge walls that surround it. Also built under his instruction was the colossal West

Angkor's rulers

802-835	Jayavarman II	1001-1002	Udayadityavarman I
835-877	Jayavarman III	1002-1049	Suryavarman
877-889	Indravarman	1050-1066	Udayadityavarman II
889-900	Yasovarman	1066-1080	Harshavarman III
900-923	Harshavarman	1080-1107	Jayavarman VI
923-928	Ishnavarman II	1107-1112	Dharanindravarman I
928-941	Jayavarman IV	1113-1150	Suryavarman II
941-944	Harshavarman II	c.1150-1165	Yasovarman II
944-968	Rajendravarman	c.1165-1177	Tribhuvanadityavarman
968-1001	Jayavarman V	1181-1218	Jayavarman VII

Baray, still in use, measuring 8 km by 2 km (so large, it can be seen from outer space) and the sanctuary atop Preah Vihear. The next in line was Udayadityavarman II (1050-1066), the son of Suryavarman I. The Baphuon temple mountain and West Mebon (in the West Baray) were built during his relatively short appointment.

Jayavarman VI (1080-1107) never settled at Angkor living instead in the northern part of the kingdom. He constructed temples outside of the main Angkor region including Wat Phou (in southern Laos) and Phimai (in Thailand). After overthrowing his great-uncle Dharanindravarman, Suryavarman II (1113-1150), the greatest of Angkor's god-kings, came to power. His rule marked the highest point in Angkorian architecture and civilization. Not only was he victorious in conflict, having beat the Cham whom couldn't be defeated by China, he was responsible for extending the borders of the Khmer Empire into Myanmar, Malaya and Siam. This aside, he was also considered one of the era's most brilliant creators. Suryavarman II was responsible for the construction of Angkor Wat, the current day symbol of Cambodia. Beng Melea, Banteay Samre and Thommanon are also thought to be the works of this genius. He has been immortalized in his own creation – in a bas-relief in the South Gallery of Angkor Wat the glorious King Suryavarman II sits on top of an elephant. After a period of political turmoil, which included the sacking of Angkor, Jayavarman VII seized the throne in 1181 and set about rebuilding his fiefdom. Historian, Dawn Rooney, suggests that Jayavarman VII was the greatest builder, "constructing more monuments, roads, bridges and resthouses than all the other kings put together."

Jayavarman VII created a new administrative centre – the great city of Angkor Thom, a 3-km block, surrounded by a moat and laterite wall. The mid-point of Angkor Thom is marked by his brilliant Mahayana Buddhist state temple, the Bayon. It is said that the Bayon was completed in 21 years. Jayavarman took thousands of peasants from the rice fields to build it, which proved a fatal error, for rice yields decreased and the empire began its decline as resources were drained. The temple consists of sculptured faces of Avolokiteshvara (the Buddha of compassion and mercy) which are often said to also encompass the face of their great creator, Jayavarman VIII. He was also responsible for restoring the Royal Palace, renovating Srah Srang and constructing the Terrace of Elephants, the Terrace of the Leper King and the nearby baray (northeast of Angkor Thom), Jayataka reservoir. At the centre of his reservoir he built Neak Pean.

Jayavarman VII adopted Mahayana Buddhism and so Buddhist principles replaced the

Hindu pantheon, and were invoked as the basis of royal authority. This spread of Buddhism is thought to have caused some of the earlier Hindu temples to be neglected. The king paid tribute to his Buddhist roots through his monastic temples: Ta Prohm and Preah Khan. Further afield in northwestern Cambodia he constructed Banteay Chhmar. He also built 102 hospitals throughout his kingdom, as well as a network of roads, along which he constructed resthouses. But because they were built of wood, none of these secular structures survive; only the foundations of four larger ones have been unearthed at Angkor.

Henri Mouhot's rediscovery of Angkor

Thai ascendency and their eventual occupation of Angkor in 1431 led to the city's abandonment and the subsequent invasion of the jungle. Four centuries later, in 1860, Henri Mouhot, a French naturalist, stumbled across the forgotten city, its temple towers enmeshed in the forest canopy. Locals told him they were the work of a race of giant gods. Only the stone temples remained; all the wooden secular buildings had decomposed in the intervening centuries. Mouhot's diaries, published in the 1860s, with his accounts of 'the lost city in the jungle', fired the imagination of archaeologists, adventurers and treasure hunters in Europe. In 1873 French archaeologist Louis Delaporte removed many of Angkor's finest statues for 'the cultural enrichment of France'.

French 'restoration'

In 1898, the École Française d'Extrême Orient started clearing the jungle, restoring the temples, mapping the complex and making an inventory of the site. Delaporte was later to write the two-volume *Les Monuments du Cambodge*, the most comprehensive Angkorian inventory of its time, and his earlier sketches, plans and reconstructions, published in *Voyage au Cambodge* in 1880 are without parallel. Henri Parmentier was chief of the school's archaeological service in Cambodia until 1930. Public interest was rekindled in the 1920s when French adventurer and novelist André Malraux was arrested in Phnom Penh, charged with stealing sculptures from one of the temples, Banteay Srei at Angkor. He published a thriller, *The Royal Way*, based on his experiences. Today around 400 sandstone, laterite and brick-built temples, walls, tombs and other structures remain scattered around the site.

Plundering of Angkor

Colonial souvenir hunters were not the first – or the last – to get their hands on Angkor's treasures. The great city's monuments were all subjected, at one time or another, to systematic plundering, mainly by the warring Cham (from South Vietnam) and Thais. Many temple pedestals were smashed to afford access to the treasure, hidden deep in pits under the central sanctuaries. Other looters knocked the tops off towers to reach the carefully concealed treasure chambers.

Centuries of entanglement in the jungle also took their toll on the buildings – strangler figs caused much structural damage and roots and vines rent roofs and walls asunder. In 1912, French writer Pierre Loti noted: "The fig tree is the ruler of Angkor today... Over the temples which it has patiently prised apart, everywhere its dome of foliage triumphantly unfolds its sleek pale branches speckled like a serpent's skin." Even today, some roots and trees remain stubbornly tangled in the ancient masonry – affording visitors a Mouhot-style glimpse of the forgotten city. Between 1953 and 1970, the Angkor

Conservancy – set up jointly by the French and Cambodian governments – maintained and restored the ruins. But when war broke out, the destructive forces of the Khmer Rouge – and other guerrilla factions – were unleashed on what the jungle had spared and the French archaeologists, such as Bernard Grosslier, had restored.

Restoration of Angkor

As if the conservation and protection of the complex was not already fraught with difficulties, a threat emerged in the mid-1980s, from the most unlikely of sources. The Vietnamese-backed administration enlisted the services of Indian archaeologists to begin where the Angkor Conservancy had left off. They were given a six-year contract to clean and restore the galleries and towers of Angkor Wat itself. Prince Sihanouk is reported to have burst into tears when he heard that the Indians, using unskilled Cambodian workmen, had begun their concrete and chemical-assisted restoration effort. The cleaning agents stripped off the patina which for a millennium had protected the sandstone from erosion by the elements. Bas-reliefs depicting scenes from the *Ramayana* were scrubbed and scraped until some were barely discernible. Cement was used with abandon. Archaeologists around the world, who, since 1970, have only been dimly aware of the rape of Angkor, now consider the gimcrack restoration programme the last straw after two decades of pillage and destruction.

Whether the Indian team of archaeologists and conservators have really caused untold damage to the monuments of Angkor through insensitive restoration and the use of untested solvents is a source of some dispute. Certainly most press reports in the West have taken the line that their work rather than helping to restore and preserve the monuments has helped to further ruin it. Cement has been used to fill in cracks, where Western archaeologists would probably have left well alone. New stone has been cut and fitted where, again, other specialists might have been happy merely to have done sufficient restoration to prevent further degeneration. The Indian team also used chemical cleaning agents – an unorthodox and contentious approach to restoration. However, although some of the methods used by the Indian team do seem rather crude and insensitive to the atmosphere of the place, the carping of some Western archaeologists seems to have been motivated as much by professional envy as anything else. The Indians were called in by the government in Phnom Penh at a time when most Western countries were boycotting the country, in protest at the Vietnamese occupation. French archaeologists in particular must have been pacing their offices in indignation and pique as a country with such 'primitive' skills took all the glory.

In 1989 UNESCO commissioned a Japanese art historian to draw up an Angkor plan of action. The top priority in its restoration, he said, was to underpin the foundations of Angkor Wat, Bayon, Baphuon, Preah Khan, Neak Khan and Pre Rup. Once the Paris Peace agreements had been signed in 1991, the Ecole Française, the New York based World Monuments Fund and the Japanese started work. UNESCO is coordinating the activities of the various teams and Angkor was declared a World Heritage site. Some temples are closed or partially closed for restoration work.

Whether the Japanese are any more sensitive than the Indians in their restoration work is an interesting subject for debate. For while the Indians may have been criticized for unsuitable techniques at least they were merely patching up. The Japanese approach is nothing less than renovation. Thus, while the traditional tools of the architect were

Who owns Angkor Wat?

The Cambodian Constitution states that all of Cambodia's heritage sites are owned by the state and its people. However, the ticketing rights to Angkor are a completely different story. Cambodia's largest corporation, Sokimex, has held ticketing rights to Angkor since 1999. The company, which runs a huge chain of Cambodian petrol stations and hotels, struck a lucrative deal with the government in May 1999. This deal has persisted until this day and is obviously very lucrative for all concerned.

From that point onward, a huge amount of myths have grown-up around the temples being owned by either Hun Sen or the Vietnamese (the owner of Sokimex is a Cambodian citizen – his partial Vietnamese ethnicity is often called into question). In fact, as stated earlier the temples are owned wholly by the people and government of Cambodia.

brushes and hammers, visitors will be surprised to see huge cranes and lifts putting temples back as Japanese archaeologists think they once looked. Concrete and laterite blocks as well as newly carved sandstone are used to replace decayed stonework. Interestingly, in 2002 Indian archaeologists were again invited back to take part in the restoration process.

Documentation of Angkor

Sanskrit and Khmer inscriptions

About 900 inscriptions have been found in Indochina that give a jigsaw set of clues to Angkor civilization. Those written in Sanskrit are largely poetic praises dedicated to gods and kings; Khmer-language ones give a much more focused insight into life and customs under the great kings. Some give a remarkably detailed picture of everyday life: one documents a ruling that pigs had the right to forage in rice fields, another dictates that ginger and honey should be used in the preparation of ritual foods. Most of the inscriptions have now been deciphered. Contemporary palm-leaf and paper documents which would have added to this knowledge have long since rotted away in the humid climate.

Bas-reliefs

Bas-reliefs carved into Angkor's temple walls also give a fascinating pictorial impression of life in the great city. Its citizens are shown warring, hunting, playing and partying and the reliefs present a picture which is often reassuringly normal in its detail: men played chess, old women read palms and people ate and drank and gossiped while musicians provided entertainment. Young men went hunting and young women evidently spent hours at the Angkorian equivalent of the hairdressers and boutiques.

Chou Ta-kuan's account

The most complete eyewitness account of Angkor was written by Chou Ta-kuan, an envoy from the Chinese court, who visited Cambodia in 1296, around 75 years after the death of Jayavarman VII, the last great conqueror of the Angkor period. Chou Ta-kuan

Angkor tips

These days avoiding traffic within the Angkor complex is difficult but still moderately achievable.

As it stands there is a pretty standard one-day tour itinerary that includes: Angkor Wat (sunrise), Angkor Thom, Bayon, etc (morning), break for lunch, Ta Prohm (afternoon), Preah Khan (afternoon) and Phnom Bakheng (sunset).

If you reverse the order, peak hour traffic at major temples is dramatically reduced. As many tour groups trip into Siem Reap for lunch this is an opportune time to catch a peaceful moment in the complex, just bring a packed lunch or eat at 1100 or 1400.

To avoid the masses at the main attraction, Angkor Wat, try to walk around the temple, as opposed to through it. Sunset at Phnom Bakheng has turned into a circus fiasco, so aim for Angkor or the Bayon at this time as they are both relatively peaceful.

Sunrise is still pretty quiet at Angkor, grab yourself the prime position behind the left-hand pond (you need to depart Siem Reap no later than 0530), though there are other stunning early-morning options, such as Srah Srang or Bakong. Bakheng gives a beautiful vista of Angkor in the early-mid morning.

wrote detailed accounts of an outsider's observations and impressions during this time. He cast Angkor as a grand and highly sophisticated civilization, despite the fact that it was, by then, well past its heyday. His descriptions of daily life actually seem quite comparable with Khmer life today. Ordinary people generally built their houses out of wood and leaves and their homes, like today, were raised on stilts. He described a society highly suspicious of evil spirits, where parents would call their children 'ugly' names, like dog, in order to deflect the attention from the evil spirits.

French interpretation

What the French archaeologists managed to do, with brilliance, was to apply scientific principles to deciphering the mysteries of Angkor. The French, and by extension the West, nonetheless managed to 'invent' Angkor for its own interests, moulding the Angkorian Empire and its art so that it fitted in with the accepted image of the Orient. (This notion that Europeans invented the Orient is most effectively argued in Edward Said's seminal book *Orientalism*, first published in 1978 and now widely available in paperback. It is a book that does not deal specifically with Angkor but much of the argument can be applied to the French appropriation of Angkor and the Khmers.) Much that has been written about the ruins at Angkor and the empire and people that built them says as much about what the French were trying to do in Indochina, as about the place and people themselves. What is perhaps ironic is that Cambodians then reappropriated the French vision and made it their own. Today, French invention and Cambodian 'tradition' are one. Cambodia, lacking the cultural integrity to resist the influence of the French, became French and in so doing they took on board the French image of themselves and made it their own.

Angkor Wat ▸▸ *For listings, see pages 61-76.*

The awe-inspiring sight of Angkor Wat first thing in the morning is something you're not likely to forget. Constructed between 1113 and 1150, it is believed to be the biggest religious monument ever built and certainly one of the most spectacular. British historian Arnold Toynbee said in his book *East to West* that: "Angkor is not orchestral; it is monumental." That sums it up. The temple complex covers 81 ha and is comparable in size to the Imperial Palace in Beijing. Its five towers are emblazoned on the Cambodian flag and the 12th-century masterpiece is considered by art historians to be the prime example of Classical Khmer art and architecture. It took more than 30 years to build and is contemporary with Notre Dame in Paris and Durham Cathedral in England. The temple is dedicated to the Hindu god Vishnu, personified in earthly form by its builder, the god-king Suryavarman II, and is aligned east to west.

Angkor Wat differs from other temples primarily because it is facing westward, symbolically the direction of death, leading many to believe it was a tomb. However, as Vishnu is associated with the west, it is now generally accepted that it served both as a temple and a mausoleum for the king. The sandstone was probably quarried from a far-away mine and floated down the Siem Reap river on rafts. Like other Khmer temple mountains, Angkor Wat is an architectural allegory, depicting in stone the epic tales of Hindu mythology. The central sanctuary of the temple complex represents the sacred Mount Meru, the centre of the Hindu universe, on whose summit the gods reside. Angkor

② **Angkor Wat**

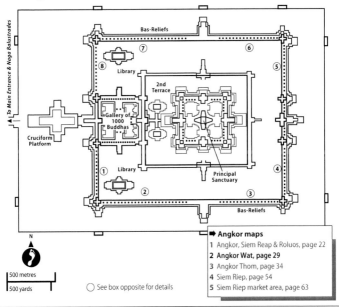

Angkor maps

Anti-clockwise round Angkor Wat's bas-reliefs

1 West gallery, southern half represents a scene from the Hindu Mahabharata epic. The Battle of Kurukshtra shows the clash between the Pandavas (with pointed headdresses, attacking from the right) and the Kauravas. The two armies come from the two ends of the panel and meet in the middle in a ferocious battle. Above the war scene is Bhima, head of the Kauravas, wounded and lying atop a pile of arrows, surrounded by grieving followers and loved ones. The centre of the sculpture reveals the chief of the Pandavas in his war chariot. (The larger the figure the more important the person.) The southwest corner has been badly damaged – some say by the Khmer Rouge – but shows scenes from Vishnu's life.

2 South gallery, western half depicts Suryavarman II (builder of Angkor Wat) leading a procession. He is riding a royal elephant and carrying an axe, giving orders to his army before leading them into battle against the Chams. Shade is provided to him by 15 umbrellas, while a gamut of servants cool him with fans. The rank of the army officers is indicated by the number of umbrellas. Other troops follow on elephants. While trailing behind them are musicians and priests bearing holy fire. The undisciplined, outlandishly dressed figures are the Thais helping the Khmers in battle against the Chams.

3 South gallery, eastern half was restored in 1946. It depicts the punishments and rewards one can expect in the afterlife. On the left-hand side, the upper and middle levels show the dead waiting for their moment of judgement with Yama (Judge of the Dead) and his assistants, Dharma and Sitragupta, as to whether they will go to either the 37 heavens or 32 hells. On the left, lead two roads one to the heavens (above), and the other to hell (below). The damned, depicted in the bottom row, are in for a rough ride: the chances of their being savaged by wild animals, seized by demons or having their tongues pulled out (or any combination thereof) are quite high. Yama was tough and some might suggest that the crime didn't exactly fit the punishment: those who damaged others' property received broken bones; gluttons were sawn in half, and those who picked Shiva's flowers had their heads nailed. The blessed, depicted in the upper two rows, are borne along in palanquins surrounded by large numbers of bare-breasted apsaras dancing on lotuses.

4 Eastern gallery, southern half, is a 50-m-long panel that's probably

Wat's five towers symbolize Meru's five peaks; the enclosing wall represents the mountains at the edge of the world and the surrounding moat, the ocean beyond.

Angkor Wat was found in much better condition than most of the other temples in the complex because it seems to have been continuously inhabited by Buddhist monks after the Thais invaded in 1431. They were able to keep back the encroaching jungle. A giant stone Buddha was placed in the hall of the highest central tower, formerly sacred to the Hindu god, Vishnu. Three modern Buddhist monasteries flank the wat.

The temple complex is enclosed by a **square moat** – more than 5 km long and 190 m wide – and a high, galleried wall, which is covered in epic bas-reliefs and has four

Angkor's best known. The Churning of the Sea of Milk, portrays part of the Hindu legend, Bhagavata-Pourana. On the North are 92 deva (gods) and on the South 88 asura (demons) battling to win the coveted ambrosia (the nectar of the gods which gives immortality).

The serpent, Vasuki, is caught, quite literally, in the centre of their dispute. The asura hold onto the head of the serpent, whilst the devas hold the tail. The fighting causes the waters to churn, which in turn produces the elixir. In the centre, Vishnu commands. Below are sea animals (cut in half by the churning close to the pivot) and above, apsaras encouraging the competitors in their fight for the mighty elixir. Eventually (approximately 1000 years later) the elixir is won by the asuras until Vishnu appears to claim the cup.

Shortly before Cambodia collapsed into civil war in 1970, French archaeologists, who were repairing the roof and columns of the east gallery, dismantled the structure. Because they were unable to finish the job, the finest bas-reliefs have been left open to the elements.
5 Eastern gallery, northern half is unfinished and depicts the garuda-riding Krishna (Vishnu's incarnation) overcoming a wall of fire, with the help of a Garuda, to claim victory over Bana, the demon king. Having captured Bana and the ambrosia, Kailasa, Parvati and Ganesh, plead with Krishna to spare Bana's life. The gate in the centre of the east gallery was used by Khmer royalty and dignitaries for mounting and dismounting elephants.
6 North gallery, eastern half shows Garuda-riding, Krishna claiming victory over the demons. Shiva is shown in meditation with Ganesh, Brahma and Krishna. Most of the other scenes are from the Ramayana, notably the visit of Hanuman (the monkey god) to Sita.
7 North gallery, western half pictures another battle scene: demons versus gods. Twenty-one gods are pictured including Varuna, god of water, standing on a five-headed naga; Skanda, the god of war (several heads and a peacock with arms); Yama, the god of dead (chariot drawn by oxen): and Suva, the sun god (standing on a disc).
8 Western gallery, northern half has another scene from the Ramayana depicting another battle between the devas and asuras – this time in the form of Rama and Ravana. The demon king Ravana, who rides on a chariot pulled by monsters and commands an army of giants, has seduced and abducted Rama's beautiful wife Sita. The battle takes place in the centre of the relief.

ceremonial tower gateways. The main gateway faces west and the temple is approached by a 475-m-long road, built along a **causeway**, which is lined with **naga balustrades**. There are small rectangular barays on either side of the roadway. To either side of the balustrades are two isolated buildings, thought to have been **libraries** – there are two more pairs of them within the temple precincts on the first and second terraces.

At the far end of the causeway stands a **cruciform platform**, guarded by stone lions, from which the devaraja may have held audiences; his backdrop being the three-tiered central sanctuary. Commonly referred to as the **Terrace of Honour**, it is entered through the colonnaded processional gateway of the outer gallery. The transitional enclosure beyond it is again cruciform in shape. Its four quadrants formed galleries, once stocked full of statues of the Buddha. Only a handful of the original 1000-odd images remain. Each gallery also had a basin which would originally have contained water for priests' ritual ablution. The second terrace, which is also square, rises from behind the **Gallery of a Thousand Buddhas**. It has a tower at each corner.

The cluster of **central towers**, 12 m above the second terrace, is reached by 12 steep stairways which represent the precipitous slopes of Mount Meru. Many historians believe that the upwards hike to this terrace was reserved for the high priests and king himself. Today, anyone is welcome but the difficult climb is best handled slowly by stepping sideways up the steep incline. The five lotus flower-shaped sandstone towers – the first appearance of these features in Khmer architecture – are believed to have once been covered in gold. The eight-storey towers are square, although they appear octagonal, and give the impression of a sprouting bud. Above the ascending tiers of roofs – each jutting gable has an elaborately carved pediment – the tower tapers into a circular roof. A quincunx shape is formed by the towers with four on each corner and another marking the centre. The central tower is dominant, and is the Siva shrine and principal sanctuary, whose pinnacle rises more than 30 m above the third level and 55 m above ground level. This sanctuary would have contained an image of Siva in the likeness of King Suryavarman II, as it was his temple-mountain. But it is now a Buddhist shrine and contains statues of the Buddha. The steps leading up to the third level are worn and very steep. On the south side the steps have a hand rail (not recommended for vertigo sufferers).

Over 1000 sq m of bas-relief decorate the temple. Its greatest sculptural treasure is the 2-m-high **bas-relief**, around the walls of the outer gallery. It is the longest continuous bas-relief in the world. In some areas traces of the paint and gilt that once covered the carvings can still be seen. Most famous are the hundreds of figures of devatas and apsaras in niches along the walls. The apsaras – the celestial women – are modelled on the god-king's own bevy of bare-breasted beauties and the sculptors' attention to detail provides an insight into the world of 12th-century haute couture. Their hair is often knotted on the crown and bejewelled – although all manner of wild and exotic coiffures are depicted. Jewelled collars and hip-girdles also are common and bracelets worn on the upper arms. Sadly many of the apsaras have been removed in recent years.

The bas-reliefs narrate stories from the *Ramayana* and *Mahabharata*, as well as legends of Vishnu, and are reminiscent of Pallava and Chola art in southeast India. Pious artisans and peasants were probably only allowed as far as Angkor Wat's outer gallery, where they could admire the bas-reliefs and pay homage to the god-king. In the open courtyards, statues of animals enliven the walls. Lions stand on guard beside the staircases. There were supposed to be 300 of them in the original building. Part of the bas-reliefs were hit by shrapnel in 1972, and some of its apsaras were used for target practice.

One of the great delights of Angkor, particularly at Angkor Wat, are the glorious trees. Huge tropical trees grow in Angkor's forests – a reminder of how much of Cambodia used to look. Driving out to Angkor from Siem Reap, the flat landscape is largely bare of trees but inside the protected area forests flourish. High in the treetops birds sing and call to each other all day. The wildlife, whose motto seems to be 'always watching: always waiting', are an integral part of Angkor. Keeping the prising tentacles and smothering creepers at bay requires constant vigilance and a sharp blade. A great deal of archaeology is still concealed in the embrace of the forest and exploring the less beaten paths often reveals some unknown and unmapped ruin.

The royal city of Angkor Thom

Construction of Jayavarman VII's spacious walled capital, Angkor Thom (which means 'great city'), began at the end of the 12th century: he rebuilt the capital after it had been captured and destroyed by the Cham. Angkor Thom was colossal – the 100-m-wide moat surrounding the city, which was probably stocked with crocodiles as a protection against the enemy, extended more than 12 km. Inside the moat was an 8-m-high stone wall, buttressed on the inner side by a high mound of earth along the top of which ran a terrace for troops to man the ramparts.

The area within the walls was more spacious than that of any walled city in medieval Europe – it could easily have encompassed the whole of ancient Rome. Yet it is believed that this enclosure, like the Forbidden City in Beijing, was only a royal, religious and administrative centre accommodating the court and dignitaries. The rest of the population lived outside the walls between the two artificial lakes – the east and west barays – and along the Siem Reap River.

Four great gateways in the city wall face north, south, east and west and lead to the city's geometric centre, the Bayon. The fifth, Victory Gate, leads from the royal palace (within the Royal Enclosure) to the East Baray. The height of the gates was determined by the headroom needed to accommodate an elephant and howdah complete with parasols. The flanks of each gateway are decorated by three-headed stone elephants and each gateway tower has four giant faces, which keep an eye on all four cardinal points.

Five causeways traverse the moat, each bordered by sculptured balustrades of nagas gripped, on one side, by 54 stern-looking giant gods and on the other by 54 fierce-faced demons. The balustrade depicts the Hindu legend of the churning of the sea (see box, page 37).

Some stone buildings survived the sacking of the city by the Cham, such as the temples of Phimeanakas and Baphuon, and these were incorporated by Jayavarman in his new plan. He adopted the general layout of the royal centre conceived by Suryavarman II.

Inside Angkor Thom

The **South Gate** provides the most common access route to Angkor Thom, predominantly because it sits on the path between the two great Angkor complexes. The gate is a wonderful introduction to Angkor Thom with well-restored statues of asuras (demons) and gods lining the bridge. The figures on the left, exhibiting serene expression, are the gods, while those on the right, with grimaced, fierce-looking heads, are the asuras. The significance of the naga balustrade, across the moat, is believed to be symbolic of a link between the world of mortals, outside the complex, to the world of gods, inside the complex. The 23-m-high gates feature four faces in a similarly styled fashion to those of the Bayon.

The **Bayon** is one of Angkor's most famous sights and most people visiting Cambodia are familiar with the beaming faces before even stepping foot in the temple. The Bayon was Jayavarman VII's own temple-mountain, built right in the middle of Angkor Thom; its large faces have now become synonymous with the Angkor complex. It is believed to have been built between the late 12th century to early 13th century, around 100 years after Angkor Wat. Unlike other Khmer monuments, the Bayon has no protective wall immediately enclosing it. The central tower, at the intersection of the diagonals city walls, indicates that the city walls and the temple were built at the same time.

The Bayon is a three-tiered, pyramid temple with a 45-m-high tower, topped by four gigantic carved heads. These faces are believed to be the images of Jayavarman VII as a Bodhisattra, and face the four compass points. They are crowned with lotus flowers,

③ **In & around Angkor Thom**

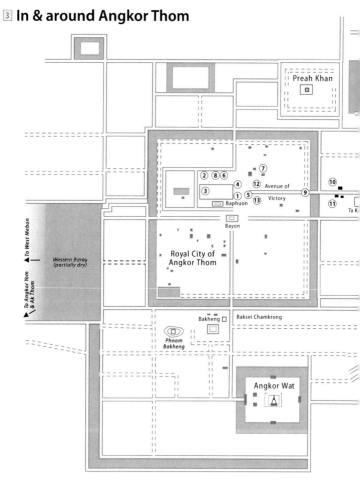

Terrace of the Elephants **1**	Tep Tranam **6**	Chau Say Tevoda **11**
Royal Enclosure **2**	Preah Pithu Group **7**	North Kleang **12**
Phimeanakas **3**	Preah Palilay **8**	South Kleang **13**
Terrace of the Leper King **4**	Victory Gate **9**	
Prasats Suor Prat **5**	Thommanon **10**	▦ Artificial lakes

800 metres
800 yards

symbol of enlightenment, and are surrounded by 51 smaller towers each with heads facing north, south, east and west. There are over 2000 large faces carved throughout the structure. Although the Bayon seems a complex, labyrinthine structure, its overall layout is quite basic. The first two of the three levels feature galleries of bas-relief (which should

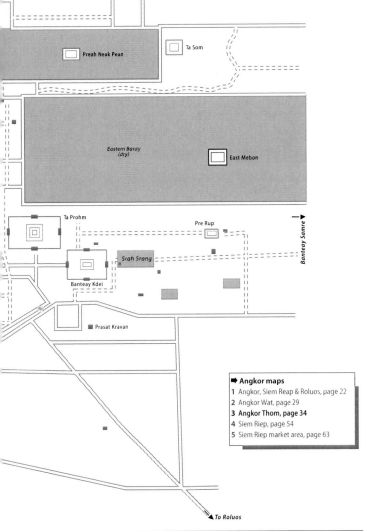

Preah Neak Pean

Ta Som

Eastern Baray
(dry)

East Mebon

Ta Prohm

Pre Rup

Srah Srang

Banteay Kdei

Banteay Samre ▶

Prasat Kravan

▶ **Angkor maps**
1 Angkor, Siem Reap & Roluos, page 22
2 Angkor Wat, page 29
3 **Angkor Thom, page 34**
4 Siem Riep, page 54
5 Siem Riep market area, page 63

▲ To Roluos

be viewed clockwise), a circular central sanctuary dominates the third level.

When Pierre Loti, the French writer, first saw these towers in 1912 he was astounded: "I looked up at the tree-covered towers which dwarfed me, when all of a sudden my blood curdled as I saw an enormous smile looking down on me, and then another smile on another wall, then three, then five, then 10, appearing in every direction". The facial features are striking and the full lips, curling upwards at the corners, are known as 'the smile of Angkor'.

Even the archaeologists of the École Française d'Extrême Orient were not able to decide immediately whether the heads on the Bayon represented Brahma, Siva or the Buddha. There are many theories. One of the most plausible was conceived in 1934 by George Coedès, an archaeologist who spent many years studying the temples at Angkor. He postulated that the sculptures represented King Jayavarman VII in the form of Avaloketsvara, the Universal Buddha, implying that the Hindu concept of the god-king had been appended to Buddhist cosmology. Jayavarman VII, once a humble monk who twice renounced the throne and then became the mightiest of all the Khmer rulers, may be the smiling face, cast in stone, at the centre of his kingdom. The multiplication of faces, all looking out to the four cardinal points, may symbolize Jayavarman blessing the four quarters of the kingdom. After Jayavarman's death, the Brahmin priests turned the Bayon into a place of Hindu worship.

The Bayon has undergone a series of facelifts through its life, a point first observed by Henri Parmentier – a French archaeologist who worked for L'École Français d'Extrême Orient – in 1924 and later excavations revealed vestiges of a former building. It is thought that the first temple was planned as a two-tiered structure dedicated to Siva, which was then altered to its present form. As a result, it gives the impression of crowding – the

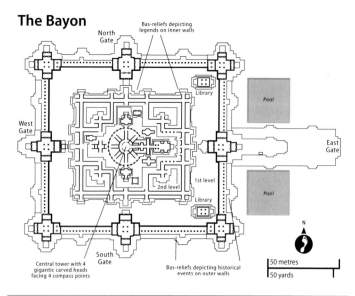

The Bayon

Bas-reliefs depicting legends on inner walls

North Gate

Library

West Gate

Pool

East Gate

2nd level

1st level

Library

Pool

N

South Gate

Central tower with 4 gigantic carved heads facing 4 compass points

Bas-reliefs depicting historical events on outer walls

50 metres

50 yards

The Churning of the Sea

The Hindu legend, the Churning of the Sea, relates how the gods and demons resolved matters in the turbulent days when the world was being created.

The elixir of immortality was one of 13 precious things lost in the churning of the cosmic sea. It took 1000 years before the gods and demons, in a joint dredging operation aided by Sesha, the sea snake, and Vishnu, recovered them all.

The design of the temples of Angkor was based on this ancient legend. The moat represents the ocean and the gods use the top of Mount Meru – represented by the tower – as their churning stick. The cosmic serpent offered himself as a rope to enable the gods and demons to twirl the stick.

Paul Mus, a French archaeologist, suggests that the bridge with the naga balustrades which went over the moat from the world of men to the royal city was an image of the rainbow. Throughout Southeast Asia and India, the rainbow is alluded to as a multi-coloured serpent rearing its head in the sky.

towers rise right next to each other and the courtyards are narrow without much air or light. When Henri Mouhot rediscovered Angkor, local villagers had dubbed the Bayon 'the hide and seek sanctuary' because of its complex layout.

The **bas-reliefs** which decorate the walls of the Bayon all seem to tell a story but are much less imposing than those at Angkor Wat. The sculpture is carved deeper but is more naive and less sophisticated than the bas-reliefs at Angkor Wat. They vary greatly in quality, which may have been because the sculptors' skills were being overstretched by Jayavarman's ambitious building programme. The reliefs on the outer wall and on the inner gallery differ completely and seem to belong to two different worlds. The relief on the outside depicts historical events; those on the inside are drawn from the epic world of Hindu gods and legends, representing the creatures who were supposed to haunt the subterranean depths of Mount Meru. In fact the reliefs on the outer wall illustrating historical scenes and derring-do with marauding Cham were carved in the early 13th century during the reign of Jayavarman; those on the inside were carved after the king's death when his successors turned from Mahayana Buddhism back to Hinduism. In total, there are over 1.2 km of bas-reliefs, depicting over 11,000 characters.

Two recurring themes in the bas-reliefs are the powerful king and the Hindu epics. Jayavarman is depicted in the throes of battle with the Cham – who are recognizable thanks to their unusual and distinctive headdress, which looks like an inverted lotus flower. The naval battle pictured on the walls of Banteay Chhmar are almost identical. Funnily enough, there's a bas-relief in the north section of the west gallery depicting a huge fish eating a deer, a complimentary inscription says "the deer is its food", an artistic directive, which the carver obviously forgot to remove. The other bas-reliefs give an insight into Khmer life at the time: the warrior elephants, oxcarts, fishing with nets, cockfights and skewered fish drying on racks; vignettes show musicians, jugglers, hunters, chess-players, people nit-picking hair, palm readers and reassuringly down-to-earth scenes of Angkor citizens enjoying a drink. In the naval battle scenes, the water around the war canoes is depicted by the presence of fish, crocodiles and floating corpses.

The **Royal Enclosure**, to the north of the Bayon, had already been laid out by Suryavarman I: the official palace was in the front with the domestic quarters behind, its gardens surrounded by a laterite wall and moat. Suryavarman I also beautified the royal city with ornamental pools. Jayavarman VII simply improved his designs.

In front of the Royal Enclosure, at the centre of Angkor Thom, Suryavarman I laid out the first Grand Plaza with the recently renovated **Terrace of the Elephants** (also called the Royal Terrace). The 300-m-long wall derives its name from the large, lifelike carvings of elephants in a hunting scene, adorning its walls. The 2.5-m wall also features elephants flanking the southern stairway. Believed to once be the foundations for the royal reception hall, lead tiles were found here in more recent years. This discovery corroborates Chinese diplomat Chou Ta-kuan's evidence that "the tiles of the king's main apartment are made of lead". Royalty once sat in gold-topped pavilions at the centre of the pavilion, and here there are rows of garudas (bird-men), their wings lifted as if in flight. They were intended to give the impression that the god-king's palace was floating in the heavens like the imagined flying celestial palaces of the gods. At the end of the terrace is an impressive sculpture of a five-headed horse. Also in front of the Royal Enclosure are the stately **North** and **South Kleangs**, which sit on the east side of the central square (opposite the Terrace of the Elephants). Although Kleang means 'storeroom', a royal oath of allegiance carved into one of the doorways indicates that they may have served as reception areas for foreign envoys. The North Kleang was originally constructed in wood under Rajendravarman II; Jayavarman V reconstructed it with stone and Jayavarman VII later added 12 laterite victory towers, called the **Prasat Suor Prat**. The function of the towers is steeped in controversy. While some say they were intended as anchors for performing acrobats and clowns, Chou Ta-kuan stated that they were used to settle disputes between performing men (to see who could last the longest seated on a tower without illness or injury). Henri Mauhot disagreed with both theories, suggesting that the towers were created to hold the crown jewels.

At the northeast corner of the 'central square' is the 12th-century **Terrace of the Leper King**, which may have been a cremation platform for the aristocracy of Angkor. Now rebuilt it is a little too fresh and contemporary for some tastes. The 7-m-high double terrace has bands of bas-reliefs, one on top of the other, with intricately sculptured scenes of royal pageantry and seated apsaras as well as nagas and garudas which frequented the slopes of Mount Meru. Above is a strange statue from an earlier date, which probably depicts the god of death, Yama, and once held a staff in its right hand. The statue's naked, lichen-covered body gives the terrace its name – the lichen gives the uncanny impression of leprosy. Opposite the Terrace of the Elephants, on the south side of the Terrace of the Leper King, are the remains of an earlier wall, carved with bas-reliefs of demons. These reliefs were found by French archaeologists and had been intentionally concealed. This illustrates the lengths to which the Khmers went to recreate Mount Meru (the home of the gods) as faithfully as possible. According to Hindu mythology, Mount Meru extended into the bowels of the earth; the bas-relief section below ground level was carved with weird and wonderful creatures to symbolize the hidden depths of the underworld. The second layer of carving is the base of Mount Meru on earth. Flights of steps led through these to the lawns and pavilions of the royal gardens and Suryavarman's palace.

The **Phimeanakas** (meaning Celestial or Flying Palace in Sanskrit) inside the Royal Enclosure was started by Rajendravarman and used by all the later kings. The structure stands close to the walls of the Royal Palace, none of which exists today. Suryavarman I rebuilt this pyramidal temple when he was renovating the Royal Enclosure. It rises from the centre of the former royal palace. Lions guard all four stairways to the central tower which was originally covered in gold, as the Chinese envoy Chou Ta-kuan related in 1296: "The king sleeps in the summit of the palace's golden tower. All the people believe that the tower is also inhabited by the Lord of the Sun, who is a nine-headed serpent. Every night the serpent appears in the form of a woman with whom the king sleeps during the first watch. None of the royal wives are allowed in the tower. The king leaves at the second watch to go to his wives and concubines. If the naga spirit does not appear one night, it is a sign that the king's death is imminent. Should the king fail to visit the naga for a single night, the welfare of the kingdom will suffer dire consequences." The Phimeanakas represented a genuine architectural revolution: it was not square, but rectangular and on the upper terrace, surrounding the central tower, there was a gallery with corbelled vaults, used as a passageway.

The **Srah Srei**, or the women's bath, to the north of Phimeanakas is also within the walled enclosure. Chou Ta-kuan appears to have enjoyed watching Angkor's womenfolk bathe, noting that, "To enter the water, the women simply hide their sex with their left hand". The Phimeanakas is linked by the **Avenue of Victory** to the Eastern Baray.

South of the Royal Enclosure and near the Terrace of the Elephants is the **Baphuon**, built by Udayadityavarman II. The temple was approached by a 200-m-long sandstone causeway, raised on pillars, which was probably constructed after the temple was built. The platform leads from the temple-mountain itself to the east gopura – an arched gateway leading to the temple courtyards. The Baphuon is not well preserved as it was erected on an artificial hill which weakened its foundations. Only the three terraces of its pyramidal, Mount Meru-style form remain and these give little indication of its former glory: it was second only to the Bayon in size. Chou Ta-kuan reported that its great tower was made of bronze and that it was "truly marvellous to behold". With extensive restoration, the temple is starting to shape-up. Most of the bas-reliefs were carved in panels and refer to the Hindu epics. Some archaeologists believe the sculptors were trying to tell stories in the same way as the shadow plays. It is believed that the fourth level wall on the western side was originally created in the form of a large, reclining Buddha, though it is hard to make out today. There is a wonderful view from the summit. South of the Baphuon, returns you back to the Bayon.

Preah Palilay, just outside the north wall of the Royal Enclosure, was also built by Jayavarman VII. Just to the east of this temple is **Tep Tranam**, the base of a pagoda, with a pool in front of it. To the east of Tep Tranam and the other side of the Northern Avenue is the **Preah Pithu Group**, a cluster of five temples.

South of Angkor Thom

Phnom Bakheng and Baksei Chamkrong
ⓘ *To get up to the ruins, either climb the steep and uneven hill where the vegetation has been cleared (slippery when wet), ride an elephant to the top of the hill (US$15) or walk up the gentle zig-zag path the elephants take.*
Phnom Bakheng, Yasovarman's temple-mountain, stands at the top of a natural hill, 60-m high, affording good views of the plains of Angkor. There is also a roped off Buddha's footprint

to see. It is just outside the south gate of Angkor Thom and was the centre of King Yasovarman's city, Yasodharapura – the 'City Endowed with Splendour'. A pyramid-temple dedicated to Siva, Bakheng was the home of the royal lingam and Yasovarman's mausoleum after his death. It is composed of five towers built on a sandstone platform. There are 108 smaller towers scattered around the terraces. The main tower has been partially demolished and the others have completely disappeared. It was entered via a steep flight of steps which were guarded by squatting lions. The steps have deteriorated with the towers. Foliate scroll relief carving covers much of the main shrine – the first time this style was used. This strategically placed hill served as a camp for various combatants, including the Vietnamese, and suffered accordingly. Today the hill is disfigured by a radio mast.

Baksei Chamkrong was built by Harshavarman I at the beginning of the 10th century and dedicated to his father, Yasovarman I. It lies at the foot of Phnom Bakheng (between Bakheng and Angkor Thom), the centre of Yasovarman's city, and was one of the first temples to be built in brick on a stepped laterite base. An inscription tells of a golden image of Siva inside the temple.

East of Angkor Thom

Chau Say Tevoda and Thommanon

There is a close group of temples just outside the east gate of Angkor Thom. Chau Say Tevoda, built by Suryavarman II, is the first temple outside the east gate and is dwarfed by Ta Keo. The temple is dedicated to Siva but many of the carvings are of Vishnu. It is similar in plan to Thommanon, next door, whose surrounding walls have completely disappeared, leaving only the gateways on the east and west ends and a ruined central tower. Originally both temples would have had a hall linked to the central tower and enclosing walls with elaborate gateways. A library, to the southeast, is the only other building in the complex. There are repeated pediments above the doorways.

Ta Keo and Ta Nei

Ta Keo, begun during Jayavarman V's reign and left unfinished, stands east of the Royal Palace and just off the Avenue of Victory. The pyramid-temple rises over 50 m, its five tower shrines supported on a five-tiered pyramid. It was one of the first temples to be built entirely of sandstone. Previous tower sanctuaries had entrances only on the east side but Ta Keo has openings on all four sides. It was originally surrounded by a moat.

Deeper in the forest, 600 m north of Ta Keo, is Ta Nei. Built by Jayavarman VII the building has appropriated the Bayon's style but on a much smaller scale. Much of the building still remains in the collapsed state but ongoing work from the Apsara Authority means the building is being used for training purposes. It is an overgrown temple with lichen-covered bas-reliefs.

Ta Prohm

For all would-be Mouhots and closet Indiana Joneses, the temple of Ta Prohm, to the south of Ta Keo, is the perfect lost-in-the-jungle experience. Unlike most of the other monuments at Angkor, it has only been minimally cleared of undergrowth, fig trees and creepers and so retains much of its mystery. Widely regarded as one of Angkor's most enchanting and beautiful temples, it is an absolute 'must-see'.

Ta Prohm was built to house the divine image of the Queen Mother and was consecrated in 1186 – five years after Jayavarman VII seized power. The outer enclosures are somewhat obscured by dense foliage but reach well beyond the temple's heart (1 km by 650 m). The temple proper consists of a number of concentric galleries featuring corner towers and the standard gopuras. Other buildings and enclosures were built on a more ad hoc basis. The temple marked the end of an architectural style in which the temple's structure lay on a single plane with rising towers alluding to the notion of elevation rather than comprising multiple levels.

It underwent many transformations and an inscription gives detailed information on the complex. Within the complex walls lived 12,640 citizens. It contained 39 sanctuaries or prasats, 566 stone dwellings and 288 brick dwellings. Ta Prohm literally translates as the Royal Monastery and that is what it functioned as, home to 18 abbots and 2740 monks. By the 12th century temples were no longer exclusively places of worship – they also had to accommodate monks so roofed halls were increasingly built within the complexes. According to contemporary inscriptions, the temple required 79,365 people for its upkeep, relying on the income of 3140 villages to subsidize the 2740 officials and 615 dancers. The list of property it owned was on an equally impressive scale. It included 523 parasols, 35 diamonds and 40,620 pearls.

The French writer Elie Lauré wrote: "With its millions of knotted limbs, the forest embraces the ruins with a violent love". Creepers entwine themselves around ancient stones like the tentacles of a giant octopus. Trunks and roots pour off temple roofs like lava flows. It was decided by the École Française d'Extrême Orient to leave the temple in its natural state. The trees are predominantly the silk-cotton tree and the aptly-named strangler fig. The plants are believed to have spawned in the temple's cracks from seeds blown in or dropped by birds. Naturally, the roots of the trees have descended towards the soil, prying their way through foundations in the process. As the vegetation has matured it has forced its way further into the temple's structure, damaging the man-built base and causing untold destruction. This has created a situation where the structures now rely on the trees for support. Herein lies the dilemma – if the trees die or are damaged, the now damaged and loose temple walls could easily crumble or collapse. Venerable trees weighing several tonnes growing on temple roofs also cause unimaginable stress, slowly shattering the stones.

In recent years a colossal tree was struck by lightening and fell on a gallery, causing quite serious damage. This reignited a campaign to 'save Ta Prohm' and a project is underway to prune some of the smaller trees and larger branches.

Banteay Kdei, Srah Srang and Prasat Kravan

The massive complex of **Banteay Kdei**, otherwise known as 'the citadel of cells', is 3 km east of Angkor Thom and just to the southeast of Ta Prohm. Some archaeologists think it may be dedicated to Jayavarman VII's religious teacher. The temple has remained in much the same state it was discovered in – a crowded collection of ruined laterite towers and connecting galleries lying on a flat plan, surrounded by a galleried enclosure. It is presumed that the temple was a Buddhist monastery and hundreds of buried Buddha statues have been excavated from the site. In recent times a community of monks has used the site but this is less common now due to the strict restrictions imposed by temple management. The temple area is enclosed by a large laterite wall, 700 m by 500 m, and has three main enclosures. Like Ta Prohm it contains a Hall of Dancers (east side), an open roof building with four separate quarters. The second enclosure runs around the perimeters of the inner enclosure. The third, inner enclosure contains a north and south library and central sanctuary. The central tower was never finished and the square pillars in the middle of the courtyard still cannot be explained by scholars. There are few inscriptions here to indicate either its name or purpose, but it is almost certainly a Buddhist temple built in the 12th century, about the same time as Ta Prohm. It is quite similar to Ta Prohm in design but on a much smaller scale. Historians Freeman and Jacques believe that it was probably built over the site of another temple. The temple is being restored, slowly but surely. However, the 13th-century vandalism of Buddha images (common to most of Jayavarman's temples) will prove a little more difficult to restore. This temple offers a few good examples of Mahayanist Buddhist frontons and lintels that escaped the desecration.

The lake or baray next to Banteay Kdei is called **Srah Srang** ('Royal Bath') and was used for ritual bathing. The steps down to the water face the rising sun and are flanked with lions and nagas. This sandstone landing stage dates from the reign of Jayavarman VII but the lake itself is thought to date back two centuries earlier. A 10th-century inscription reads 'this water is stored for the use of all creatures except dyke breakers', ie elephants. This design is believed to be characteristic of that adopted in the Bayon. The Baray, which measures 700 m by 300 m, has been filled with turquoise-blue waters for over 1300 years. With a good view of Pre Rup across the lake, some archaeologists believe that this spot affords the best vista in the whole Angkor complex. The green landscape around the baray and beautiful views offer a tranquil and cool resting place, perfect for a picnic lunch.

On the road between Angkor Wat and Banteay Kdei, on the small circuit, is **Prasat Kravan**. The temple, built in AD 921, means 'Cardamom Sanctuary' and is unusual in that it is built of brick. (By that time brick had been replaced by laterite and sandstone.) It consists of five brick towers arranged in a line. The bricklayers did a good job, especially considering they used a vegetable composite as their mortar. The temple's bas-reliefs are considered a bit of an anomaly as brick was hardly ever sculpted upon. In the early 10th century, temples were commissioned by individuals other than the king; Prasat Kravan is one of the earliest examples. It was probably built during the reign of Harshavarman I.

The Hindu temple, surrounded by a moat, is positioned in a north-south direction. Two of the five decorated brick towers contain bas-reliefs (the north and central towers). The central tower is probably the most impressive and contains a linga on a pedestal. The sanctuary's three walls all contain pictures of Vishnu; the left-hand wall depicts Vishnu disguised as Vamana the dwarf. The incarnation of Vamana was used to dupe the evil demon king, Bali, into letting the unassuming dwarf take a small space to meditate. Instead the mighty Vishnu rose up, taking three important steps – from a pedestal, across the ocean, to a lotus – in order to reclaim the world from the evil demon king. On the right-hand wall again is the mighty Vishnu riding his Garuda. Common to both the bas-reliefs is the four-armed Vishnu waving around a number of objects: disc, club, conch shell and ball – these are all symbolic of his personal attributes and power. On the opposing wall is Vishnu, this time with eight arms standing between six rows of people meditating above a giant reptile.

The Northern tower is devoted to Lakshimi, Vishnu's wife. Like her consort, she is also baring her personal attributes. The best light to view the relief is in the morning.

The Cardamom Sanctuary is named after a tree that grew on the grounds. Ironically, its ruin has been largely due to the roots of trees growing beneath it. The French have been involved in the temple's reconstruction. The temple's twin, Prasat Neang Khamau (the Black Lady Sanctuary), can be found outside Phnom Penh.

Pre Rup

Northeast of Srah Srang is Pre Rup, the State Temple of King Rajendravarman's capital. Built in AD 961, the temple-mountain representing Mount Meru is larger, higher and artistically superior than its predecessor, the East Mebon, which it closely resembles. In keeping with the tradition of state capitals, Pre Rup marked the centre of the city, much of which doesn't exist today. The pyramid-structure, which is constructed of laterite with brick prasats, sits at the apex of an artificial, purpose-built mountain. The temple is enclosed by a laterite outer wall (127 m by 117 m) and inner wall (87 m by 77 m) both which contain gopuras in the centre of each wall. The central pyramid-level consists of a three-tiered, sandstone platform, with five central towers sitting above. This was an important innovation at Pre Rup and East Mebon, that the sanctuary at the top was no longer a single tower – but a group of five towers, surrounded by smaller towers on the outer, lower levels. This more complicated plan reached its final development at Angkor Wat 150 years later. The group of five brick towers were originally elaborately decorated with plaster, but most of it has now fallen off. However, the corners of each of the five towers contain guardian figures – as per tradition, the eastern towers are female and the western and central towers are male. The shrine has fine lintels and columns on its doorways. But the intricate sandstone carvings on the doors of the upper levels are reproductions. The upper levels of the pyramid offer a brilliant, panoramic view of the countryside.

Eastern Baray, East Mebon and Banteay Samre

The **Eastern Baray** – or Baray Orientale – was built by Yasovarman I and fed by the Siem Reap River. This large reservoir (7 km by 1.8 km), now dried up, was the labour of love for Yasovarman I. Historian Dawn Rooney believes it took 6000 workers more than three years to complete. The baray was Yasovarman I's first major work. To keep the punters on side he needed to provide a reliable water supply to his new kingdom, Yasodharataka. And that he did. At full capacity the baray could hold around 45-50 million cu m of water. He named the baray Yasodharataka and declared it protected by the goddess Ganga (overseen by abbots from the ashramas south of the baray). The four corners are marked by stelae.

Today, a boat isn't required to reach the middle of the Eastern Baray, where the flamboyant five towers of the **East Mebon** are located. Intrepid traveller Helen Churchill Candee remarked of the temple: "Could any conception be lovelier, a vast expanse of sky-tinted water as wetting for a perfectly ordered temple."

The Hindu pyramid structure consists of three tiers. Guarding the corners of the first and second levels are carefully sculpted elephants and sculptures (the best one is in the southeast corner). The inner enclosure contains eight smaller towers and skilfully carved lintels upon the gopuras featuring Lakshmi being watered down by two elephants and Vishnu in his man-lion guise, Narasimha. The upper terrace contains the five towers, the northwest tower features Ganesha riding his own trunk; the southeast tower shows an elephant being eaten by a monster and the central sanctuary's lintels depict Indra on his mount and Varuna the Guardian.

Finished in AD 952, Rajendravarman seems to have followed the Roluos trend and dedicated East Mebon to his parents. The East Mebon and Pre Rup were the last monuments in plaster and brick; they mark the end of a Khmer architectural epoch. The overall temple construction utilizes all materials that were available at the time: plaster, brick, laterite and sandstone. Although many believe East Mebon to be a temple-mountain, that wasn't its original intention, it just appears that way now that surrounding waters have disappeared. The Siem Reap River is said to have been diverted while the temple was built.

Banteay Samre lies further to the east, around 500 m past the east end of the East Baray. It is a Hindu temple dedicated to Vishnu, although reliefs decorating some of the frontons (the triangular areas above arches) portray Buddhist scenes. It is thought to have been built by Suryavarman II and has many characteristics of Angkor Wat such as stone-vaulted galleries and a high central tower. The bas-reliefs are in fine condition.

North of Angkor Thom

Preah Khan

Northeast of the walled city of Angkor Thom, about 3.5 km from the Bayon, is the 12th-century complex of Preah Khan. One of the largest complexes within the Angkor area, it was Jayavarman VII's first capital before Angkor Thom was completed. The name Preah Khan means 'sacred sword' and probably derives from a decisive battle against the Cham, which created a 'lake of blood', but was inevitably won by Jayavarman VII.

Preah Khan is not uniform in style. It is highly likely that Jayavarman VII's initial very well-organized and detailed city plans went slightly pear-shaped during the working city's life. A number of alterations and buildings were added, in addition to a vast civilian habitation (huts and timber houses), which all came together to create a complex labyrinth of architectural chaos. It is similar in ground plan to Ta Prohm (see page 40) but attention was paid to the approaches: its east and west entrance avenues, leading to ornamental causeways, are lined with carved stone boundary posts. Evidence of 1000 teachers suggests that it was more than a mere Buddhist monastery but most likely a Buddhist university. Nonetheless an abundance of Brahmanic iconography is still present on site. Around the rectangular complex is a large laterite wall surrounded by large garudas wielding the naga (each over 5 m in height). The theme continues across the length of the whole 3-km external enclosure, with the motif dotted every 50 m. Within these walls lies the surrounding moat.

The city is conveniently located on the shores of its own baray, Jayataka (3.5 km by 900 m). Some foundations and laterite steps lead from the reservoir, where two beautiful gajasimha lions guard the path. It is best to enter the temple from the baray's jetty in order to experience the magnificence of the divinities and devas of the Processional Way (causeway leading across the moat).

The construction's four walls meet in the centre creating two galleries and likewise, two enclosures. The outer enclosure contains the traditional four gopuras (adorned with stately bas-reliefs) and the Hall of Dancers. This hall contains an elaborate frieze of dancing apsaras and was used, in recent times, to host charity performances to help fund the area's restoration. Within the enclosure there are also a few ponds, libraries and supplementary buildings, most notably, a two-storey pavilion (north of the performance hall) which is believed to have housed the illustrious 'sacred sword'.

The second and innermost walls run so closely together that it is possible to pass through the following enclosure without realizing you had entered it (this is probably due to an expansion undertaken very early on in the piece to offer additional protection to the shrines).

The inner enclosure is a bewildering array of constructions and shrines. Holes in the inner walls of the central sanctuary of Preah Khan suggest they may once have been decorated with brass plates – an obvious target for looters. One inscription implies that up to 1500 tonnes was used within the edifice. The temple was built to shelter the statue of Jayavarman VII's father, Dharanindravarman II, in the likeness of Bodhisattva Avatokitsvara, which has now probably been smashed. A stela was discovered at the site glorifying the builder, Jayavarman VII and detailing what it took to keep the place ticking over. The inventory mentions that for Preah Khan's upkeep, the services of 97,840 men and women, 444 chefs, 4606 footmen and 2298 servants were required. Preah Khan's inscriptions also refer to the existence of 515 other statues, 102 royal hospitals of the kingdom, 18 major annual festivals and 10 days' public holiday a month.

The temple was starting to deteriorate, but clearing and careful conservation have helped remedy this. During the dry season, the World Monuments Funds (WMF), based in New York, undertakes archaeological site conservation activities here.

Preah Khan

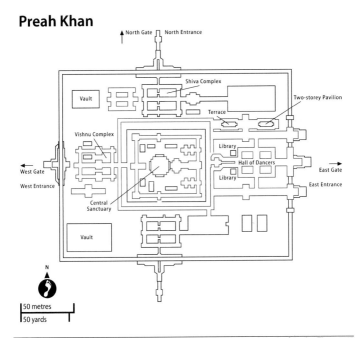

Preah Neak Pean, Ta Som and Krol Ko

To the east of Preah Khan and north of the Eastern Baray are two more Buddhist temples built by Jayavarman VII: Preah Neak Pean (the westernmost one) and the ruins of Ta Som. The exquisite temple of **Neak Pean** was also a fountain, built in the middle of a pool, representing the paradisiacal Himalayan mountain-lake, Anaavatapta. Two nagas form the edge of the island and their tails join at the back. In modern Khmer it is known as the *Prea-sat neac pon* – the 'tower of the intertwined dragons'. The colossal image of the horse is the compassionate Bodhisattva who is supposed to save sailors from drowning. The temple pools were an important part of the aesthetic experience of Preah Khan and Neak Pean – the ornate stone carving of both doubly visible by reflection. Such basins within a temple complex were used for religious ritual, while the larger moats and barays were used for bathing, transport and possibly for irrigation.

Located north of the East Baray is the pretty **Ta Som**. This mini temple has many of the same stylistic and design attributes of Ta Prohm and Banteay Kdei but on a much smaller scale. Unlike the larger constructions of Jayavarman VII, Ta Som's layout is extremely simple – three concentric enclosures and very few annex buildings. The main entrance is to the east, which would indicate some urbanization on the eastern side of the temple. The two inner enclosures are successively offset to the west. The outer (third) enclosure (240 m x 200 m) is pierced by two cruciform gopuras; the eastern one is preceded by a small terrace bound by naga balustrades. The current entry is through the western gopura as this faces the road between East Mebon and Preah Neak Pean and cuts across the moat.

Krol Ko sits north of Preah Neak Pean and about 2 km past Ta Som. The tower was built in the late 12th to early 13th century. Referred to as the Oxen Park, Krol Ko is a single, laterite tower which is about 30 m sq. The two frontons represent bodhisattva Lokesvara, to whom it is believed the temple is dedicated.

West of Angkor Thom

Western Baray, West Mebon and Ak Thom

ⓘ *Take Highway 6 west. About 3 km west of the airport turning a track leads north. It is 4 km from Highway 6 to Western Baray. Boats can be hired from the beach on the south of the Western Baray. The boat trip to West Mebon takes about 15 mins.*

The **Western Baray** was built by Udayaditavarman II possibly to increase the size of the irrigated farmlands. In the centre, on an island, is the West Mebon, where the famous bronze statue of Vishnu was discovered (now in the National Museum at Phnom Penh). Today, the eastern end of the Western Baray is dry but the scale remains astonishing, more than 2 km across and 9 km long with an average depth of 7 m. It is believed that the reservoir could hold around 123 million cubic litres of water.

South of the Western Baray is **Ak Thom**, marking the site of Jayavarman II's earlier city. It is the oldest surviving temple in the Angkor region and although little remains, it is worth a visit. The central towers are constructed mostly of brick cemented together with a mortar of vegetable sap, palm sugar and termite soil.

Outlying temples

It is possible to visit the other ancient Khmer sites dotted around the main temples at Angkor. Most of these temples can be reached by motos (motorbike taxi) or by car.

The Roluos Group

The Roluos Group, some 16 km southeast of Siem Reap, receives few visitors but is worth visiting if time permits. Jayavarman II built several capitals including one at Roluos, at that time called Hariharalaya. This was the site of his last city and remained the capital during the reigns of his three successors. The three remaining Hindu sanctuaries at Roluos are **Preah Ko**, **Bakong** and **Lolei**. They were finished in AD 879, AD 881 and AD 893 respectively by Indravarman I and his son Yashovarman I and are the best preserved of the early temples.

All three temples are built of brick with sandstone doorways and niches. The use of human figures as sculptural decoration in religious architecture developed around this time – and examples of these guardian spirits can be seen in the niches of Preah Ko and Lolei. Other sculptured figures which appear in the Roluos Group are the crouching lion, the reclining bull (Nandi – Siva's mount) and the naga. The gopura – an arched gateway leading to the temple courtyards – was also a contemporary innovation in Roluos. Libraries used for the storage of sacred manuscripts appeared for the first time, as did the concentric enclosures surrounding the central group of towers. Preah Ko and Lolei have characteristics in common: both were dedicated to the parents and grandparents of the kings who built them. Neither temple has a pyramid centre like Bakong as the pyramid temples were built exclusively for kings.

Preah Ko, meaning 'sacred ox', was named after the three statues of Nandi (the mount of the Hindu god, Siva) which stand in front of the temple. Orientated east-west, there is a cluster of six brick towers arranged in two rows on a low brick platform, the steps up to which are guarded by crouching lions while Nandi, looking back, blocks the way. The front row of towers was devoted to Indravarman's male ancestors and the second row to the female. The ancestors were represented in the image of a Hindu god. Only patches remain of the once magnificent stucco relief work, including a remnant of a kala – a motif also found on contemporary monuments in Java.

Indravarman's temple-mountain, **Bakong**, is a royal five-stepped pyramid temple with a sandstone central tower built on a series of successively receding terraces with surrounding brick towers. It may have been inspired by Borobudur in Java. Indravarman himself was buried in the temple. Bakong is the largest and most impressive temple in the Roluos Group by a long way. A bridge flanked by a naga balustrade leads over a dry moat to the temple. The central tower was built to replace the original one when the monument was restored in the 12th century and is probably larger than the original. Local children will point out to you that it is just possible to catch a glimpse of Angkor Wat from the top. The Bakong denotes the true beginning of classical Khmer architecture and contained the god-king Siva's lingam. The most important innovations of Indravarman's artists are the free-standing sandstone statues – such as the group of three figures, probably depicting the king with his two wives, who are represented as Siva with Uma, a Hindu goddess and consort of Siva, and Ganga, goddess of the Ganges River. The corners of the pyramid are mounted with statues of elephants and the steps guarded by crouching lions. Nandi watches the steps from below. The heads of all the figures are now missing but the simplicity of the sculpture is nonetheless distinctive; it is a good example of early Khmer craftsmanship. The statues are more static and stockier than the earlier statues of Chenla. There is now a Buddhist monastery in the grounds – originally it was dedicated to Siva.

Lolei was built by Yashovarman I in the middle of Indravarman's baray. The brick towers were dedicated to the king's ancestors, but over the centuries they have largely disintegrated; of the four towers two have partly collapsed. Much of the decoration has worn away but the inscriptions carved in the grey sandstone lintels and door jambs remain in good condition.

Phnom Krom and Phnom Bok

Today, Phnom Krom, 12 km southwest of Siem Reap, is the base for nearby boat trips out to the Tonlé Sap's floating villages. However, at the top of the 140-m-high mountain, stands a ruined temple believed to have been built in the late 9th-10th century by Yasovarman I but there are no inscriptions giving exact details. The square laterite enclosure (50 m by 50 m) features a gopura in the middle of each outer wall and includes 10 halls, now mostly crumbled, that make an almost continuous inner square. On a lower platform are three stone sanctuary towers, aligned north to south, dedicated to Shiva, Vishnu and Brahma. The temple affords amazing 360-degree panoramic views, which extend across to the Western Baray and Tonlé Sap's floating villages.

Phnom Bok is the brother temple to Phnom Krom and features almost an identical layout to Phnom Krom. The carvings and decorative features here remain in far better condition due to their more protected location and relatively recent discovery. Approximately 15 km northwest of Siem Riep, the temple sits at the pinnacle of the 235-m-high hill. It is the most elevated of the three temple peaks of Angkor; with Phnom Krom at 137 m and Phnom Bakheng at only 60 m (the hill that is climbed the most by tourists being by far the smallest). All three temples were built by Yasovarman I; Phnom Bakheng was the first.

The ascent of Phnom Bok is a difficult climb but well rewarded, as the 20- to 30-minute hike up the southern slope reveals a limitless horizon, broken only to the north by the view of Phnom Kulen.

Banteay Srei ('Citadel of Women')

ⓘ *It is 25 km from Ta Prohm along a decent road and takes about 35-40 mins by motorbike. The way is well signed. There are lots of food and drink stalls.*

Banteay Srei, to the north of Angkor, is well worth the trip. This remarkable temple was built by the Brahmin tutor to King Rajendravarman, Yajnavaraha, grandson of Harshavarman (AD 900-923), and founded in AD 967. The temple wasn't discovered until 1914, its distance from Angkor and concealment by overgrown jungle meaning that it wasn't picked up in earlier expeditions. At the time of discovery, by geographic officer Captain Marec, the site was so badly damaged that mounds of dirt had covered the main structure and foliage had bored its way through much of the site. It wasn't until 1924 that the site was cleared and by 1936 it had been restored.

Banteay Srei translates as 'Citadel of Women', a title bestowed upon it in relatively recent years due to the intricate apsara carvings that adorn the interior. While many of Angkor's temples are impressive because of their sheer size, Banteay Srei stands out in the quality of its craftsmanship. The temple is considered by many historians to be the highest achievement of art from the Angkor period. The explicit preservation of this temple reveals covered terraces, of which only the columns remain, which once lined both sides of the primary entrance. In keeping with tradition, a long causeway leads into the temple, across a moat, on the eastern side.

The main walls, entry pavilions and libraries have been constructed from laterite and the carvings are in pink sandstone. The layout was inspired by Prasat Thom at Koh Ker. Three beautifully carved tower-shrines stand side by side on a low terrace in the middle of a quadrangle, with a pair of libraries on either side enclosed by a wall. Two of the shrines, the southern one and the central one, were dedicated to Siva and the northern one to Vishnu. Both had libraries close by, with carvings depicting appropriate legends. The whole temple is dedicated to Brahma and many believe this temple is the closest to its Indian counterparts. Beyond this inner group of buildings was a monastery surrounded by a moat.

In 1923 controversy surrounded the temple when it was targeted by famous French author André Lalraux for a major looting expedition. The author of *The Royal Way* (1930) shamefully attempted to pillage Banteay Srei of its treasures, having read that the temple not only contained a series of brilliant carvings in excellent condition but that it was also unexcavated (which he took to mean abandoned). He travelled to Angkor and proceeded to cut out one tonne of the finest statues and bas-reliefs. Fortunately, he was arrested trying to leave the country with the treasures and was sentenced to three years in prison (a term that he did not serve). One of the best known statues from this site is a sculpture of Siva sitting down and holding his wife, Uma, on his knee: it is in the National Museum of Arts in Phnom Penh.

Having been built by a Brahmin priest, the temple was never intended for use by a king, which goes some way towards explaining its small size – you have to duck to get through the doorways to the sanctuary towers. Perhaps because of its modest scale Banteay Srei contains some of the finest examples of Khmer sculpture. Finely-carved pink sandstone ornaments roofs, pediments and lintels, all magnificently decorated with tongues of flame, serpents' tails, gods, demons and floral garlands.

Phnom Kulen

It takes a good 2 hrs by moto to get to Phnom Kulen from Siem Reap; it is more than 1 hr beyond Banteay Srei. At the height of the wet season the road will be virtually impassable. Entering the park costs foreigners an extra US$20 (or US$12 from the Angkor City Hotel beforehand) plus a fee for a motorbike or car (US$25-30) and it is not covered by the Angkor ticket scheme.

Phnom Kulen – or Mount Mohendrapura – 28 km northeast of Angkor and 48 km from Siem Reap, is a sandstone plateau considered sacred by the Khmers. The site is the mythical birthplace of the Cambodian Kingdom. At the hill's summit is the largest reclining Buddha in the country – over 900 years old. Jayavarman II built his first brick pyramid temple-mountain – to house the sacred golden Siva-lingam – here at the beginning of the ninth century. Today the temple is only visible in fragments although, over a millennium later, the phallic emblem is said to be still on display in the Phnom Kulen complex. The temple is best known for its carved lintels and bas-reliefs. There are also some remains of ninth-century Cham temples in the area.

Today the hill is clothed in forest and the nights here are cold and the days fresh and invigorating. As with most of the other sites on Phnom Kulen it is necessary to have a guide to point them out as they are small and well concealed in the forest. Khmer visitors to the area seem only to be interested in the reclining Buddha.

Phnom Kbal Spean ✗

ⓘ *Kbal Spean is 50 km northeast of Siem Reap and should cost no more than US$10 by moto (last entry 1530). Upon arrival, follow the path for 1.5 km for about 40 mins up the narrow path. The ideal time to visit is at the end of the wet season, when the fast flowing water gushes around, but doesn't submerge most of the carvings.*

The intriguing spot of Kbal Spean is rich in both style and purpose. The name of the river, and the mountain from which it springs, translates loosely to Headwater Bridge, referring to a natural sandstone arch, marking the beginning of the 150 m of carvings, upstream from the bridge. It is the downstream part, from the bridge to the waterfall, that gives the river its Sanskrit name Sahasralinga, 'River of a Thousand Lingas'.

Phnom Kbal Spean is regarded as highly auspicious so it is not surprising that the remarkable 11th-century riverbed rock carvings display a gallery of gods and celestial beings including Vishnu reclining on the serpent Anata, Shiva, Brahman, Lakshmi, Rama and Hanuman. Some of the carvings are submerged by the river, while a few have been hacked away by unscrupulous looters. The visibility of all carvings is really dependent on the time of year.

Downstream from the carvings are thousands of sculpted lingas in the river bed and a large underwater representation of a yoni (womb). The lingas stretch approximately 6 m downstream from the bridge, to 30 m upstream. Carved from the coarse sandstone from the riverbed, some protrude as much as 10 cm from the bed; others have been worn away by the flowing water. Finnish journalist Teppo Turkki, who visited the site for the *Phnom Penh Post*, wrote at the beginning of 1995: "The lingas, some of which date back to the ninth century, are about 25 cm sq and 10 cm deep and lined in a perfect grid pattern. The river runs over them, covering them with about 5 cm of pristine water." He continued: "The holy objects are designed to create a 'power path' for the Khmer kings." More likely the water which would have fed Angkor was being sanctified before it entered the holy arena of the temples. Beyond the series of carvings is a 15-m waterfall to a crystal-clear pool.

Chau Srei Vibol

ⓘ *Turn east off the road from between Phnom Bok and Roluos, about 5 km south of Phnom Bok. Follow the road over several old bridges until you reach the compound of Wat Trach and the laterite wall at the bottom of the hill.*

The remote, 11th-century hilltop temple of Chau Srei Vibol is now in ruins but at least three major sandstone structures, a sanctuary and two libraries with decorative carvings, are readily identifiable. A couple of broken lions flank the steep eastern entrance gate.

Whilst viewing this small ruined temple in near silence it's worth reflecting on the building boom that occurred under the reign of Suryavarman I, a highpoint in the Khmer Empire. Suryavarman ruled a huge empire, covering much of southern Vietnam, Thailand, Laos and the Malay Peninsula.

Beng Mealea

ⓘ *Beng Mealea is a full day trip from Siem Reap. There is an entrance fee of US$20.*
Beng Mealea, a huge 12th-century temple complex, 40 km east of the Bayon and about 7 km southeast of Phnom Kulen, is completely ruined even though it was built at about the same time as Angkor Wat. Its dimensions are similar but Beng Mealea has no central pyramid. It is widely believed that this temple acted as the 'blueprint' for Angkor. Most of the Buddhist temples built under Jayavarman VII – Preah Khan, Banteay Kdei, Ta Som and Ta Prohm – were modelled after this complex.

Further temples of interest include Sambor Prei Kup, see page 57; Preah Khan, see page 59 and Koh Ker, see page 59.

Anlong Veng and around → *For listings, see pages 61-76.*

From the outset Anlong Veng seems like your average Cambodian dusty, one-street frontier town with a towering mountain range in its midst. But the façade is deceiving. This small, unassuming town was once home to some of the country's most dangerous residents including Pol Pot, his right-hand man, Son Sen and Ta Mok, otherwise known as the "Butcher". These days the place gets a pretty bad rap by locals and expats alike but does have its merits: the people, for the most part, are tremendously friendly and it's surrounded by beautiful countryside and very hospitable rural villages. The town is also a good launching pad for a trip to Preah Vihear Temple, as the road between Anlong Veng and the temple is in relatively good shape (in the dry season).

Sights
There aren't many 'tourist' attractions per se but the town will appeal to those interested in Khmer Rouge history as it contains a number of sites decisive to the movement's downfall. The most popular destination around Anlong Veng is **Oh Chit**, Ta Mok's hauntingly beautiful lake, which was initially built as a moat for his house. A maniacal dam builder, Ta Mok (aka Brother Number Three) flooded much of the area while trying to develop the lake. Today the dead tree stumps, tranquil waters, grassy knolls and beautiful patches of lotus flower actually create a very beautiful but eerie atmosphere. On any given day packs of small kids swim in the lake while beneath the surface it is believed that the grisly remains of hundreds of people lie. You can visit **Ta Mok's Villa** ⓘ *US$2, which includes entrance to Pol Pot's residence*, the Khmer Rouge's last official headquarters after Pol Pot was overthrown. It was also the place where Pol Pot was tried by his own men, led by Ta Mok. The villa is quite barren these days, looted by government officials, but still

bares a few horrific reminders of the old days, including animal-like cages where prisoners were held captive. Inside the building there is a map marking Khmer Rouge territory and a few utopian paintings of Cambodia through the eyes of the regime. Across the lake is **Pol Pot's residence** (now reduced to a bathroom) accessed by a turn-off on the right further from town on the same road heading north, where he was kept under house arrest under Ta Mok's direction. Some of the people working at the site are former Khmer Rouge, employed by Ta Mok. The villa and lake can be accessed by following the main road through town and turning right at the signpost.

About 8 km along Anlong Veng's main street is the bottom of **Dongrek mountain range**. The Dongrek Enscarpment is a site in itself, with spectacular, panoramic views from the cliffs over to Thailand, however, half way up the mountain is an old **Khmer Rouge checkpoint**. Here there are several life-size sculptures of Khmer Rouge troops (with AK47S, kramas and grenades). Considering that the Khmer Rouge were not purveyors of artistic culture these sculptures are particularly detailed (and headless since the government decapitated them). As you move further along this road a small military house marks a path to **Pol Pot's cremation site**, where in 1998 he was burnt on a pyre of rubbish. The gravesite is accessible and marked although a sombre lonely place. (Try and stay to the marked path as some of this area remains mined.) Strangely enough some Khmers visit the site in the belief that winning lottery numbers will be bestowed upon them by greater forces. There will probably be a government official on site procuring some sort of entrance fee.

Further along in the mountains, in a heavily mined area, are the former homes of Pol Pot, Son Sen and Ta Mok, all in close proximity to the border in case a quick get-away was required. It is probably no coincidence that the modern day houses of Nuon Chea and Khieu Samphan also sit on the Thai border, near Pailin. Thankfully, when the time came for their arrest, they were unable to use any escape route.

Siem Reap and around

The nearest town to Angkor, Siem Reap is a bustling tourism hub with a growing art and fashion crowd, however it's still true to say that without the temples few people would ever find themselves here. Siem Reap is also an easy place to stay for volunteers looking to do a stint in saving the world, but perhaps too many nights spent in crowded bar street distracts from the task in hand. Visitors exhausted by the temple trail might care to while away a morning or afternoon in Siem Reap itself. The town has developed quite substantially in the past couple of years and, with the blossoming of hotels, restaurants and bars, it is now a pleasant place in its own right. Hotel building has pretty much kept pace with tourist arrivals so the town is a hive of activity.

The town is laid out formally and because there is ample land on which to build, it is pleasantly airy. Buildings are often set in large overgrown grounds resembling mini wildernesses. The current level of unprecedented growth and development is set to continue, so this may not be the case five years from now. The growth spurt has put a great strain on the city's natural resources.

Ins and outs → *For listings, see pages 61-76.*

See under the Angkor section, page 7.

Sights

The town proper has a romantic, French colonial feel, sprawling across a 10 km radius and carved apart by a pleasant lamp-lit river. The most popular tourist areas are around the Old Market (Psah Chas), the Wat Bo part of town and along the Airport Road.

The **Old Market** area is the most touristed part of the town with a gamut of restaurants, bars and boutiques catering for a wide range of tastes. Staying around here is recommended for independent travellers and those staying more than two or three days. A fair proportion of the buildings around here, particularly on the road south to Tonlé Sap, are built of wood and raised off the ground on stilts. (The distance from Siem Reap to the edge of the lake fluctuates by many kilometres; the highest water levels occurring

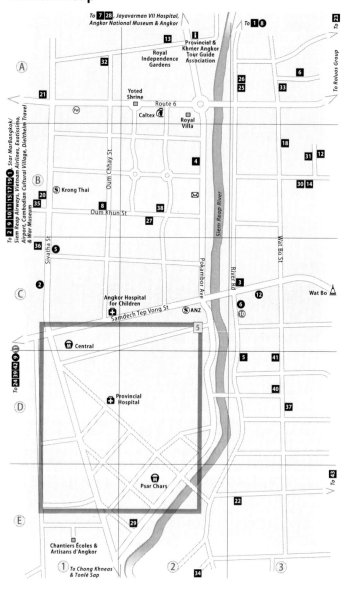

4 Siem Reap

To 7 28, Jayavarman VII Hospital, Angkor National Museum & Angkor

To 1 8

To 23

To Roluos Group

13

Provincial & Khmer Angkor Tour Guide Association

Royal Independence Gardens

32

A

26
25

33

6

21

Yoted Shrine

Route 6

Caltex

Royal Villa

18

Pol

31 12

4

30 14

To 2 9 10 11 15 17 19 1 Star Mar Bangkok/ Siem Reap Airways, Vietnam Airlines, Exotissimo, Airport, Cambodian Cultural Village, Dieltheim Travel & War Museum

B

Krong Thai

Oum Chhay St

20

35

8

38

Oum Khun St

27

36

5

Siem Reap River

Wat Bo St

C

2

Angkor Hospital for Children

Samdech Tep Vong St

ANZ

3

12

6
10

Wat Bo

Pokambor Ave

River Rd

5

Central

To 24 39 42 9 11

5

41

D

Provincial Hospital

40

37

To 43

Psar Chars

E

22

29

Chantiers Écoles & Artisans d'Angkor

1 To Chong Khneas & Tonlé Sap

2

3

34

N

100 metres
100 yards

Sleeping 🛏
Angkor Palace Resort
 & Spa **17** A1
Angkor Village Resort **1** A3
Aspara Angkor **2** A1
Bopha **5** D3
Bou Savy **19** B1
Borann **6** A3
Casa Angkor **8** B1
Earthwalkers **10** B1
Empress Angkor **11** B1
European Guesthouse **12** B3
FCC Angkor **4** B2
Golden Banana B&B **34** E2
Green Garden Home
 Guesthouse **35** B1
Heritage Suites **23** A3
Home Sweet Home **14** B3
Jasmine Lodge **15** B1
Kazna **24** C1
La Noria **26** A3
La Residence D'Angkor **3** C3
Le Meridien Angkor **7** A2
Mahogany Guesthouse **18** B3
Mekong Angkor Palace **36** C1
Neak Pean **20** B1
Ombrelle & Kimono **37** D3
Passaggio **22** E3
Paul Dubrule **9** B1
Raffles Grand Hotel d'Angkor
 13 A2
Rosy Guesthouse **25** A3

Royal Bay Inn Angkor
 Resort **38** B2
Salabai **39** D1
Shadow of Angkor II **40** D3
Shinta Mani **27** B2
Sokha Angkor **21** A1
Sofitel Royal Angkor **28** A1
Soria Moria **41** D3
Sweet Dreams
 Guesthouse **31** B3
Ta Prohm **29** E2
Two Dragons Guesthouse
 30 B3
Victoria Angkor **32** A1
The Villa **42** D1
Villa Kiara **43** E3
Yakhom Angkor
 Lodge **33** A3

Eating 🍴
Abacus **1** B1
Barrio **2** C1
Butterflies Garden **12** D3
Curry Walla **5** C1
L'Oasi Italiana **8** A3
Moloppor Café **6** C3
Sugar Palm **9** D1

Bars & clubs 🍸
Fresh at Chilli Si Dang **10** C3
Zone One **11** C1

towards the end of October at the end of the wet season.)

Across the river, the area has taken on the name of Siem Reap's oldest pagoda, **Wat Bo** (built in the 18th century), which can be found at the end of Achamean Street. This area has recently become a popular place to stay with a range of accommodation available. It's not as crowded as the old market area and less traffic than airport road.

The **Airport Road** area has been earmarked for mass tourism and wields countless cumbersome hotels and chains, geared towards package tourists, with packaged meals and packaged tours to go. You can still get into town from these hotels but it is a fair hike, especially at night. Still, this area holds appeal for those that want to fly in and out of Siem Reap and visit Angkor without sticking around for too long.

Yet while Siem Reap is a pleasant enough place to hang out for a few hours, the main places of interest lie outside the town. On the road 6 km south of Banteay Srei temple is the small **landmine museum** ⓘ *0730-1730, US$2; follow the Angkor Wat road north out towards Banteay Srei and you will find the museum on the right hand-side*. The museum exhibits a vast collection of defused mines, bombs, ammunition and other ordinance. Former deminer, Mr Akira, commendably opened the museum in 1997 to create awareness about the insidious effect of mines and help fund his work with landmine victims. When on site, he goes to great lengths to explain the carnage caused by each type of mine (such as what part of the body they are aimed at) and often speaks openly of his experiences as a child conscript during the Khmer Rouge period and later Vietnamese occupation.

On the Airport Road, near the airport, is the **War Museum** ⓘ *daily 0730-1730, US$3.*

This government-run museum houses a collection of old tanks, guns and other war paraphernalia collected from the provinces. It's not as absorbing as the mine museum but is worth a trip for those interested in war artillery and machinery.

Cambodian Cultural Village ⓘ *6 km from Siem Reap on the Airport Rd, T063-963098, daily 0900-2100, US$12*, is a park featuring smaller renditions of ancient Cambodian architectural feats and models, slightly on the kitsch side, of the various ethnic housing styles. The traditional dancing and wedding shows will be a hit if you have children with you.

There is now an **Angkor National Museum** ⓘ *daily 0830-1800, US$12, www.angkornationalmuseum.com*, on the road to the temples a short walk from the town centre. Due to the high entry price this museum is usually empty and it does seem rather incongruous that the artefacts on display here are not actually still in situ at the temples themselves. Having said that this isn't a bad museum and a lot of useful information about the development of Angkor can be gathered from here. There are also some intriguing background details such as the 102 hospitals built during the reign of Jayavarman VII and the 1960 boxes of hemorrhoid cream that were part of their annual provisions. There are also some displays of what clothes the average Angkorian wore but it's a shame there isn't more about the daily lives of these ancients.

Tonlé Sap

The Tonlé Sap, the Great Lake of Cambodia, is one of the natural wonders of Asia. Uniquely, the 100-km-long Tonlé Sap River, a tributary of the mighty Mekong, reverses its flow and runs uphill for six months of the year. Spring meltwaters in the Himalayas, coupled with seasonal rains, increase the flow of the Mekong to such an extent that some is deflected up the Tonlé Sap River. From June the lake begins to expand until, by the end of the rainy season, it has increased in area four-fold and in depth by up to 12 m. At its greatest extent, the lake occupies nearly a seventh of Cambodia's land area, around 1.5 million ha, making it the largest freshwater lake in Southeast Asia. From November, with the onset of the dry season, the Tonlé Sap River reverses its flow once more and begins to act like a regular tributary – flowing downhill into the Mekong. By February the lake has shrunk to a fraction of its wet season size and covers 'just' 300,000 ha.

This pattern of expansion and contraction has three major benefits. First, it helps to restrict flooding in the Mekong Delta in Vietnam. Second, it forms the basis for a substantial part of Cambodia's rice production. And third, it supports perhaps the world's largest and richest inland fishery, yielding as much as 10 tonnes of fish per square kilometre. It is thought that four million people depend on the lake for their subsistence and three out of every 4 kg of fish caught in the country come from the Tonlé Sap.

Because of the dramatic changes in the size of the lake some of the fish, such as the 'walking catfish', have evolved to survive several hours out of water, flopping overland to find deeper pools. *Hok yue* – or elephant fish – are renowned as a delicacy well beyond Cambodia's borders. Large-scale commercial fishing is a major occupation from February to May and the fishing grounds are divided into plots and leased out. Recent lack of dredging means the lake is not as deep as it was and fish are tending to swim downstream into the Mekong and Tonlé Sap rivers. The annual flooding covers the surrounding countryside with a layer of moist, nutrient-rich mud which is ideal for rice growing. Farmers grow deep-water rice, long-stalked and fast growing – it grows with the rising lake to keep the grain above water and the stem can be up to 6 m long. The lake also houses people, with communities living in floating villages close to the shore.

Chong Khneas ① *boats can be hired and trips to floating villages are offered, expect to pay about US$10-15 per hr; take a moto from Siem Reap (US$2), boats from Phnom Penh berth at Chong Khneas*, is 10 km south of Siem Reap. This consists of some permanent buildings but is a largely floating settlement. The majority of the population live in houseboats and most services – including police, health, international aid agencies, retail and karaoke – are all provided on water. A trip around the village is testimony to the ingenuity of people living on this waterway with small kids paddling little tubs to each other's houses.

Chong Khneas gets hundreds of visitors every day. For a more authentic, less touristy experience head out a bit further, 25 km east, to the village of **Kompong Phluk**. Costs to get to these villages are pretty high (up to US$50 per person) but are brought down if there are more passengers on the boat. See **Terre Cambodge** or **Two Dragon's Guesthouse** under Activities and tours to organize a tour.

Also on the Tonlé Sap Lake is the **Prek Toal Biosphere** – a bird sanctuary which is home to 120 bird species, including cranes, stalks and pelicans. Boats can be organized from Chong Kneas to visit the Prek Toal Environment Office, US$30 return, one hour. From here you can arrange a guide and another boat for around US$20. **Terre Cambodia**, www.terrecambodge.com, runs boat tours upwards of US$80, as do **Osmose**, T012-832812, osmose@bigpond.com.kh, and the **Sam Veasna Center for wildlife and conservation**, T063-761597, info@samveasna.org. There is basic accommodation at the Environment Office.

Kompong Thom and around → *For listings, see pages 61-76.*

Kompong Thom is Cambodia's second largest province and the provincial capital is more like a city than a town. It can be quite chaotic as it is a major thoroughfare for people going to Siem Reap and the regions further north. The town was severely bombed by the USA in the 1970s and large craters spotted in the area are testament to this. The Sen River divides the town into two distinct areas with the compact city area to the south and a more sprawling, industrial area to the north. There are plenty of sites to explore around town including the magnificent former capital, Sambor Prei Kuk and Phnom Santuk.

Sambor Prei Kuk

① *Motos will do the return trip for US$8-10, tuk tuks about US$12 and taxis for US$25 per car. There is a great route (about 1 hr) via some beautiful rural villages, rice paddies and farming lots; follow NH6 towards Siem Reap for 5 km until the road veers into a much worse road, NH64 (the road to T'Beng Meanchey); follow this for another 10 km and turn right at the big colourful archway and follow the road through to the temples (another 19 km). There are food and drink stalls within the temple complex on the main road. A small entrance fee, US$3 per person is charged at the tourist information centre at the complex gates and you are required to pay extra to take the bike through.*

Sambor Prei Kuk is a group of over 100 temples which lies 28 km north of Kompong Thom. This ancient Chenla capital, dating from the seventh century, was built by King Ishanavarman I (AD 616-635) and dedicated to Shiva. Sambor Prei Kuk is believed by many to be Southeast Asia's first temple city. The main temples are square or octagonal brick tower-shrines on high brick terraces with wonderful ornamentation in sandstone, especially the lintel stones. The finely sculptured brick has an obvious Indian influence, for example the use of lion sculptures, an animal which didn't exist in Cambodia. The temples are divided into three geographical groups: the Prasat Sambor Group, the Prasat Tao Group and the Prasat Yeay Peu Group. All of the temples are dedicated to Shiva. Some highlights include the inner lingas in the temples of the Prasat Sambor Group (try looking up from the sanctuary to the sky); and the lions guarding the temple of Prasat Tao (unfortunately they are reproductions).

It is believed that there were originally between 180 and 200 monuments but many of these were completely shattered during the US bombardment and craters left by American bombing during the war are still visible. Paradoxically, even the park's conservation centre has been destroyed, so much so that one can consider it as one of Sambor Prei Kuk's ruins. However, given that these are some of the oldest temples in the country – 200 years before Angkor was built, they are well preserved and now that the area is safe, they are really worth visiting, especially for the the forested solitude they afford. There are some amazing trees, some which look as old as the structures themselves. Botanists have been through the area and have put little identification signs on most foliage. There is a tranquil atmosphere and very few visitors, unlike Angkor.

Phnom Santuk

① Motos that congregate around the taxi stand and Arunreas Hotel will do the trip 20 km southeast of Kompong Thom for US$5-6 (roundtrip).

The 980 steps to the pagoda at the top of Phnom Santuk Mountain is a great trip to do around noon in order to later catch the brilliant sunset and stunning panoramic views of the countryside. The holy mountain is the most significant in the region and around the brightly painted pagoda are some fascinating Buddha images carved out of large stone boulders. Though many tourists might see the temple as a bit garish or kitsch, the site is hugely popular with the Khmers, who believe it to be somewhat auspicious. There are several vendors around the area, including a gamut of people touting traditional medicines and therapies.

T'Beng Meanchey and around → *For listings, see pages 61-76.*

T'Beng Meanchey is a small, dusty, non-descript town whose future hinges on the development of the roads between the remote temple sites of Koh Ker, Preah Khan and Preah Vihear – if this happens, in all likelihood it will become a major gateway to these remote temples. At the time of writing only a dribble of tourists were making it here, and the place has a more remote feel than areas such as Ban Lung or Sen Monorom. Aside from being a 'gateway' to major temples in the region, T'Beng Meanchey also pierces the junction of some of the country's worst roads. However, the good news is that the roads are being overhauled courtesy of an Asian Development Bank loan so hopefully this will change in years to come.

Sights

The town itself doesn't have a whole lot of tourist attractions apart from the Joom Noon Silk Project and Wat Chey Preuk. The **Joom Noon Silk Project** is a local initiative started by

Vietnam veteran, Bud Gibbons, to help rehabilitate people with disabilities through silk weaving projects. These days Bud has handed over the reins to internationally acclaimed weaver, Carol Cassidy. This organization can be credited with producing some of the country's finest silk products which are available nationwide. The **Wat Chey Preuk** compound is almost opposite the hospital. It includes the few remaining structures of an ancient Pre-Angkorian temple built on the site, though it really isn't worth a trip out of your way to see.

Preah Khan

ⓘ *Visiting Preah Khan is a long day trip for die-hard motorcyclists or temple enthusiasts. It is not easy as the sandy roads make for a very uncomfortable trip there. A very early start is required to make it there and back to T'Beng Meanchey in a day. It is advisable to take a mosquito net, hammock and torch (which can be hung in the temple) in case you get stuck out here for the night. Only walk on well-trodden tracks as the area is still heftily mined. There is a small village about 5 km from the site where it is possible to pick up a drink or snack. There are no official guides.*

Preah Khan ('sacred sword'), known as 'Bakan' to most locals, ranks as one of the most remote temples in Cambodia. Surrounded by dense foliage that's presumably speckled with mines and near-impassable roads, a trip to Preah Khan is not for the faint-hearted. Its development is highly mysterious, though most believe that the complex was built in the ninth century and was home to both Suryavarman II and Jayavarman VII at some point (possibly during the Cham invasion). The temples were originally built for Hindu worship and later were transformed into a Buddhist complex. Scholars believe that the laterite and sandstone complex is the largest single enclosure ever constructed during the Angkor period, even superseding the mighty Angkor Thom. Preah Khan was originally linked to Angkor Wat via an ancient super-highway constructed of laterite and there are a number of fantastically carved stone bridges between the two points that still exist today.

The first temple most will see on approach is Prasat Preah Stung, with the Jayavarman VII trademark of large Bayon-like smiling faces peering out over the jungle. To the east is a massive 3-km-long baray and east of this is a petite ninth-century temple, Prasat Preah Damrei. This intricate pyramid is also known as Elephant Temple due to the two regal carved elephants gracing it. The main temple structure is now in ruins and is about 400 m from Prasat Preah Stung. Disappointingly, this temple has been so severely looted that no semblance of its former glory exists whatsoever and much of the building, aside from the outer walls, has collapsed upon itself. Looting has long been a problem here: the recidivist French looter, Louis Delaporte, carted off thousands of kilograms of artefacts to the Guimet Museum in Paris and recently a couple of looters were killed when part of the building collapsed on them. The main structure is in a ruinous state and it's hard to distinguish many of its features as a result, though some bas-reliefs on the outer walls are quite good.

Cows graze freely within the temple's walls and exploring the temples has a real Indiana Jones-caught-in-the-middle-of-nowhere feel. You'll usually have the temples to yourself, aside from a few inquisitive village children.

Koh Ker

ⓘ *Kulen, 32 km away, is the closest village to Koh Ker. You can also access Koh Ker from Siem Reap via Beng Melea. A new toll road has been established which makes the 61 km from Beng*

Melea, and 146 km from Siem Reap, a breeze. If hiring a car or moto for this trip expect to pay upwards of US$50 and US$30 respectively.

Koh Ker (pronounced *Koh Care*) is the site of the old capital of Jayavarman IV (AD 928-942). Historians today still do not understand exactly why Jayavarman IV moved the capital from Angkor to Koh Ker, but after a feud with his family the capital was relocated. One inscription reads of Jayavarman IV and Koh Ker "founded by his own power, a city which was the seat of prosperities of the universe". It was a short-lived prosperous seat of the universe, however, as Koh Ker only remained the capital for 24 years. The main ruin here is **Prasat Thom**, an overgrown, seven-storey, stepped period in a pyramid style. The surrounding land was irrigated by baray, similar to, but smaller than, the ones at Angkor. The **Rahal Baray**, east of the pyramid, is 1200 m long by 560 m wide and made out of existing stone. The sculptors used sandstone for most of their carvings and were able to create great detailed scenes of movement that were not previously created in this era. Many of the carvings, such as the fighting monkey men, are now kept in the National Museum of Phnom Penh. De-miners have been working a lot in this area and it is believed that over 80 ruined temples lie in the area.

Ankor and around listings

For Sleeping and Eating price codes and other relevant information, see Essentials page 11.

🛏 Sleeping

Anlong Veng *p51*

There is quite a lot of accommodation on the main road in town.

$ 23 October Guesthouse (or Questhouse as it is misprinted on their business card), right at the roundabout past **Lucky Star** and on the opposite side of the road, T012-228993. Concrete building and lacking atmosphere.

$ Bot Oddom Guesthouse, right at the only roundabout on the main road just after the police HQ on left hand side, T012-779495. In addition to the typical local guesthouse with US$7 rooms there is a new modern-style hotel with large public balcony areas with views over Ta Mot's lake and the mountainous border. Up to US$15 with a/c, these are large rooms with 2 double beds and TV. Recommended.

$ Dorng Rek Hill Accommodation, literally on the hill looking out over the Cambodian plains, T012-444067. This isolated spot is an unusual place to stay, but the views are worth it. Rooms are basic, with Khmer-style shower in the en-suite bath rooms. Unfortunately, the building itself is not very aesthetic with its surroundings.

$ Lucky Star, right at the only roundabout on the main road just after the police HQ on right hand side. Newly built looking like a US motel with more than 40 rooms. Has the **New Lucky** restaurant next door and rooms have a/c.

$ Monorom Guesthouse and Restaurant, on the main road towards the lake, T011-766428. Rooms are very clean and include a/c, fan, attached bathroom, free water and a pineapple! In the middle of expansion at time of printing, so currently a little disorganized, but should be ready at the end of 2010.

$ Pnom Dorngrek Guesthouse, T092-228847. With rooms starting at US$400 this place is not too bad, it has a real local feel as if you are staying with a family and is adorned with family wedding portraits. It is home to many dogs. Rooms are a little pokey but are clean and have a fan. Rooms with attached Western-style bathroom are also available.

$ Sokha Rith Guesthouse, on main road over the roundabout towards lake, T017-242404. Typical Khmer decor and clean with option of a/c or fan rooms.

Siem Reap *p53, maps p54 and p63*

Hotel accommodation in Siem Reap has expanded dramatically in the past couple of years reflecting the huge surge in demand.

Accommodation is spread across 3 main areas – east of the river in **Wat Bo Village** (cheaper accommodation), on the **airport road** (luxury hotels and others that cater to package tourists), and around the **Old Market** (the main bar and restaurant area). There are also quite a few hotels on the road to Angkor.

It is not uncommon for taxi, moto and tuk tuk drivers to tell new arrivees that the guesthouse they were booked into is now closed or full. They will try to take you to the place where they get the best commission. One way around this is to arrange for the guesthouse or hotel to pick you up from either the bus station or other arrival point – many offer this service for free or a small fee.

Town centre and east of river

$$$$ Angkor Village Resort, T063-963561, www.angkorvillage.com. Opened in 2004, the resort contains 80 rooms set in Balinese- style surroundings. The accommodation pays homage to traditional Asian architecture with lovely fittings, especially in the bathrooms. Traditional massage services, 2 restaurants, theatre shows and lovely pool. Elephant, boat and helicopter rides can be arranged. Recommended.

$$$$ FCC Angkor, near the post office on Pokambor Av, T063-760280, www.fcc cambodia.com. The sister property of the famous FCC Phnom Penh this is a cute hotel set in the grounds of a restored, modernist villa. Rooms offer contemporary luxury and plenty of space but be warned – there is a massive generator at one end of the complex running 24/7 so make sure you are housed well away from here. Also tends to trade more on its reputation so service and food can be decidedly ropey.

$$$$ Heritage Suites, behind Wat Po Lanka, T063-969100, www.heritage.com.kh. Super luxurious and exclusive villas, rooms and suites in this stylish property secreted away behind a temple. Much is made with traditional materials and the top-end rooms come with private steam baths and gardens. A super-splurge but well worth it. Expect all the usual amneties for such a top-end establishment.

$$$$ La Residence D'Angkor Hotel, River Rd, T063-963390, www.residence angkor.com. With its beautifully laid out rooms all lavishly furnished with marble and hardwoods this reassuringly expensive hotel could persuade the most principled among us to sell their souls to the corporate beast. Each room has a huge, free-form bathtub – which is the perfect end to a day touring the temples. The pool is lined with handmade tiles in a variety of green hues and, like the rest of the hotel, is in true Angkor style. This and the Victoria hotel go head-to-head as offering the best room in town.

$$$$ Le Meridien Angkor, Charles de Gaulle Blvd, Khum Svay Dang Hum (main road towards temples), T063-963900, www.lemeridien.com/angkor. From the outside this 5-star hotel resembles a futuristic prison camp – severe, angled architecture with small, dark slits for windows. Walk into the lobby and it is immediately transformed into space and light, becoming, in a flash, a pretty decent place to lay your hat. Rooms are nicely designed and sized and all come with a/c, en suite and cable TV. Other facilities include spa, restaurants and pool. The garden is a lovely spot to take breakfast. Recommended.

$$$$ Raffles Grand Hotel d'Angkor, 1 Charles de Gaulle Blvd, T063-963888, www.raffles.com. Certainly a magnificent period piece from the outside, Siem Reap's oldest (1930) hotel fails to generate ambience, the rooms are sterile and the design of the huge new wings is uninspired (unforgivable in Angkor). Coupled with this is a history of staff lock-outs and mass sackings that have caused the Raffles brand damage. However, it does have all the mod-cons, including sauna, tennis, health and beauty spa, lap pool, gym, 8 restaurants and bars, nightly traditional performances, landscaped gardens, 24-hr valet service and in-house movie channels. Disappointing.

$$$$ Royal Bay Inn Angkor Resort, Oum Khon St, T063-760500, www.royalbayinn angkor.com. All rooms have balconies facing onto a huge swimming pool in this new resort, set in nice gardens. Expect the usual upmarket trimmings of a/c, multi-channel TV and good service.

$$$$ Shinta Mani, Oum Khum and 14th St, T063-761998, www.shintamani.com. This 18-room boutique luxury hotel is wonderful in every way: the design, the amenities, the food and the service. The hotel also offers a beautiful pool, library and has mountain bikes available. Provides vocational training to under-privileged youth. Listed in *Gourmet Magazine* as one of the 'World's Best Hotel Dining Rooms'. Recommended. At time of writing this hotel is undergoing major re-furbishment and is due to re-open early 2011.

$$$$ Sofitel Royal Angkor, Charles de Gaulle Blvd, T063-964600, www.sofitel.com. A large 238-room hotel in a garden-like setting, a large attractive swimming pool and 5 restaurants (including Asian, International and French) and bars. Other perks include an open-air jacuzzi, health and beauty spa. Rates include buffet breakfast and dinner. Not as intimate as some of the other hotels in this price range.

$$$$ Sokha Angkor, Sivatha St, T063-969999, www.sokhahotels.com. One of the few Cambodian-owned 5-star hotels in the country, the rooms and services here are top notch, even if the decor is a little gaudy (if you can't afford to stay here, do come and check out the incredibly over-the-top swimming pool, complete with faux temple structures and waterfalls). Also home to an excellent Japanese restaurant. Recommended.

$$$$ Victoria Angkor Hotel, Route 6, T063-760428, www.victoriahotels-asia.com. Perfection. A beautiful hotel with that 1930s, East-meets-West style that exemplifies the French tradition of Art de Vivre. The superb facilities make you feel like you are staying in another era – each room is beautifully

2 Siem Reap market area

➡ **Angkor maps**
1 Angkor, Siem Reap & Roluos, page 22
2 Angkor Wat, page 29
3 Angkor Thom, page 34
4 Siem Riep, page 54
5 Siem Riep market area, page 63

Sokimex Mini Mart
Central
DHL
Angkor Web
Cambodia Commercial
Lao Airlines
Sivatha St
Provincial Hospital
Kokoon Store
Happy Cambodia
Traditional Khmer Massage
Senteurs d'Angkor
Night Market
ATS
Union Commercial
Psar Chars
CCB
Pokambor Ave
Blue Apsara Bookshop
Canadia

N
50 metres
50 yards

Sleeping ▭
Hotel de la Paix **5**
Jim's Place **2**

Eating 🍴
Blue Pumpkin **1**
Curry Walla II **2**
Molly Malone's **3**
Neth Socheata **4**
Shadow of Angkor I **6**
Steung Siem Reap **7**
Dead Fish Tower **5**
Khmer Kitchen **3**
Le Malraux **4**
Le Tigre de Papier **6**
Red Piano **7**
Singing Tree **8**
Soup Dragon **11**
Tell **12**

Bars & clubs 🍸
Angkor What? **13**
Laundry **14**
Linga **15**
Miss Wong **9**
Temple Club **16**
Warehouse **10**
X Rooftop Bar **17**

decorated with local fabrics and fantastic furniture (some Japanese style others more Indian). Swimming pool, open-air salas, jacuzzi and spa. It's the small touches and attention to detail that stands this hotel apart from the rest. Highly recommended.

$$$$ Villa Kiara, just outside eastern edge of town, Sala Kamroeuk village, T063-764156, www.villakiara.com. Set in a very peaceful, private garden compound a couple of kilometres east of town this 17 room/suite "boutique" resort is unpretentious yet stylish. There's free breakfast, Wi-Fi, a restaurant and complimentary transfers to and from town. The pool is cute as well. All rooms are, of course, a/c with TV and en suite hot-water facilities. Recommended.

$$$ Borann, T063-964740, borann@ bigpond.com.kh. Attractive hotel in a delightful garden with a pool. A short way down a quiet lane it is secluded and private. 5 small buildings each contain 4 comfortable rooms with terracotta floors and a lot of wood. Some rooms have a/c, some fan only: price varies accordingly. Restaurant.

$$$ Casa Angkor, corner of Oum Chhay St and Oum Khun St, T063-966234, www.casa angkorhotel.com. This is a good looking, pleasant and well-managed 21-room hotel in a central location. 3 classes of room, all a decent size, well appointed and with cool wooden floors. Friendly reception and efficient staff. Restaurant, beer garden and reading room. Like all Siem Reap hotels this one offers the full range of tour services, airport run, etc.

$$$ Kazna Hotel, market end of Taphul Rd, T063-969313, www.kaznahotel.com. Decent, clean well-run mid-range hotel in good location. Every room has a/c and private hot-water bathrooms, TV and rate includes Wi-Fi and breakfast. The better, pricier rooms have balconies. Nice wooden floors and intriguing colour schemes add to the vibe.

$$$ La Noria, on road running on east side of the river, just past the 'stone' bridge,

T063-964242, www.lanoriaangkor.com. Almost perfect riverside setting for this gorgeous small resort. Tranquil gardens, a small pool and a real away-from-it-all vibe seduces guests who stay in brightly coloured a/c and en suite rooms each with their own balcony. No TV, very quiet and decent restaurant. Recommended.

$$$ Ombrelle & Kimono, 557 Wat Bo Rd. T09-2774313, www.ombrelle-et-kimono.com. Only 5 rooms in this minute villa complete with pool and arty gardens. The rooms are a little pretentious but the welcome is friendly. All en-suite, a/c and with private terrace.

$$$ Passaggio, near the Old Market, T063-760324, www.passaggio-hotel.com. 15 double and 2 family rooms, spacious, a/c, minibar and cable TV, internet, laundry service, bar and restaurant, outdoor terrace.

$$$ Soria Moria, Wat Bo Rd, T063-964768, www.thesoriamoria.com. Excellent, well-run small hotel that has a rooftop bar and a decent restaurant. Rooms – all en suite, with contemporary Asian flourishes, a/c and colour TVs – are quiet, and the upper ones have nice airy views over the town. Highly recommended.

$$ Bopha, on the east side of the river, slightly up from Passagio, T063-964928, bopharesa@everyday.com.kh. Stunning hotel. Good rooms with all the amenities, decorated with local furniture and fabrics. Brilliant Thai-Khmer restaurant.

$$ Golden Banana Bed and Breakfast, Wat Damnak Area (past Martini Bar), T012-885366, info@golden-banana.com. Good, clean rooms and decent restaurant.

$$ Home Sweet Home, T063-963245, sweethome@camintel.com. Popular guest-house and a favourite of the moto drivers (who get a kickback). Regardless, it is still quite good accommodation. Good clean rooms, some with TV and a/c.

$$ Mekong Angkor Palace Hotel, 21 Sivatha Rd, T063-963636, www.mekongangkor palaces.com. Excellent mid-range hotel in good central location. All of the spotless rooms, are trimmed with a contemporary Khmer vibe, free Wi-Fi, a/c, hot-water bathrooms and TVs. Room rates also include breakfast and there's an excellent swimming as well. Great value and recommended.

$$ Salabai, 155 Taphul Rd, T063-963329, www.salabai.com. Part of an NGO programme that trains disadvantaged young Cambodians to work in the hospitality industry. The rooms are decent enough, in a good location and the suite is an excellent deal. Cheaper rooms have fan, pricier ones a/c, all have private hot water showers. Gets booked up so reserve in advance.

$$ Shadow of Angkor II, Wat Bo Rd, T063-760363, www.shadoworangkor.com. Set on quiet Wat Bo Rd this is the sister guesthouse of **Shadow of Angkor I** located on the market side of the river. This is another place offering well-located, good-value, well-run mid-range accommodation. As well as being clean and comfortable most rooms have balconies and all have a/c, free Wi-Fi, TVs and hot water.

$$ The Villa, 153 Taphul St, T063-761036, www.thevillasiemreap.com. From the outside this place looks like a funky little guesthouse but some of the rooms are small and dark. All have a/c, TV and shower while the more expensive deluxe rooms are spacious and spotless.

$$ Two Dragons Guesthouse, Wat Bo Village, T012-868551, www.twodragons-asia.com. Well-run mid-range budget guesthouse. All the spotless rooms come with a/c, private en suite hotwater facilities, cable TV and free Wi-Fi. They also pride themselves on giving up-to-date information about everything and anything Siem Reap.

$$ Yaklom Angkor Lodge, Wat Bo St, T012-983510, www.sawasdee-angkor.com. An attractive site and friendly, competent staff who speak good English. The 10 small, simple bungalows are built slightly too close, together. Try to negotiate a discount. Breakfast and airport transfer included. **Sawasdee Thai** restaurant.

$ European Guesthouse, T012-582237 www.european-guesthouse.com. 12 fan rooms in a quiet lane off Wat Bo St occupied by 3 guesthouses.

$ Green Garden Home Guesthouse, down a small lane off Sivatha St, T012- 890363. Price varies according to facilities required. A/c or fan, hot water or cold water, etc, cable TV. Garden not as great as their PR would suggest.

$ Mahogany Guesthouse, Wat Bo St, T063-963417/012-768944, proeun@big pond.com.kh. Fan and now some a/c. An attractive and popular guesthouse, lovely wooden floor upstairs (try to avoid staying downstairs), coffee-making facilities and a friendly crowd of guests.

$ Rosy Guesthouse, east side of river before **Noria**, T063-965059, www.rosy guesthouse.com. Good, clean rooms with bathroom. Very popular.

$ Sweet Dreams Guesthouse, off Wat Bo St, T012-783013, homesweet home@every day.com.kh. Clean and well-kept rooms in this small guesthouse in a quiet cul-de-sac. A favourite of the motos who obviously get a commission for bringing you here. Restaurant.

Around the Old Market (Psar Chars)

$$$$ Hotel de la Paix, corner of Achemean and Sivatha, T063-966000, www.hotelde lapaixangkor.com. Owned by the same company that also runs Bangkok's famous **Bed Supper Club**, this is probably Siem Reap's best-value luxury hotel. The rooms offer simple contemporary design with giant bathtubs and plump bedding – all a/c and with cable TV. The pool is a maze of plinths and greenery and makes for a perfect spot to laze. Can feel a bit urban for Siem Reap but still a great hotel. Recommended.

$$$$ Steung Siem Reap Hotel, St 9, T063-965167, www.steungsiemreaphotel.com. This new-build colonial-era-styled hotel is an excellent addition to the central market area of Siem Reap. The pleasant rooms come with cooling wooden floors and many overlook a verdant and very quiet swimming pool. There are all the trimmings you'd expect in this price range, including gym, sauna, free Wi-Fi and free breakfast, a/c, huge bathtubs and good, friendly service. Recommended.

$$$ Molly Malone's, across from **Red Piano** in Old Market area, T063-963533. Fantastic rooms with 4-poster beds and good clean bathrooms. Irish pub downstairs. Lovely owners. Recommended.

$$$ Neak Pean, 53 Sivatha St, T063- 924429, neakpean @camintel.com. 100 rooms, many in large wooden bungalows behind the main building. Swimming pool and garden. Large restaurant.

$$$ Ta Prohm, T063-380117, www.angkor hotels.org/ta_prohm_hotel. 95 large rooms in a well-kept and long-established property overlooking the river. Bathroom with bathtub. It is a touch overpriced but fair by Siem Reap standards. From the outside it can be difficult to tell whether the hotel is actually open but it is. Restaurant and tourist services.

$$ Shadow of Angkor I, 353 Pokambor Av, T063-964774, www.shadowofangkor.com. Big old colonial-era house, overlooking the river, the better rooms have balconies, a/c, hot water, and TV. The cheaper rooms, while equally spotless, come with fans. There is also free Wi-Fi and a communal terrace to sit and ponder the river. Run by the same friendly Khmer family who own its sister hotel across the river, **Shadow of Angkor II**.

$ Jim's Place, St 9, T063-764005, www.jim place.net. Every room here comes with hot water, en suite bathrooms, cable TV, a/c and free Wi-Fi. They are spotless, though basic but some have rather eccentric toilet designs. Friendly and in good location.

$ Neth Socheata, 10, St 2 Thnou, T063-963294, www.angkorguesthouseneth socheata.com. One of the Siem Reap's best deals, this small newly built budget guesthouse, tucked away down a quiet small alley opposite the market, has very nice, clean, pleasantly decorated rooms. All have en suite hot-water facilities and the price varies according to if you choose a/c or fan. The best rooms have small balconies while others are windowless. There's free Wi-Fi and a friendly welcome. Recommended.

On the airport road

The numbers of hotels springing up here are hard to keep track of. Most of them are also aimed at Korean, Chinese and Japanese package tourists, so facilities, food and even languages spoken will reflect this.

$$$$ Angkor Palace Resort & Spa, Airport Rd, T063-760511, www.angkorpalace resort.com. Set back from the road in huge, private gardens this is one of the better choices for upmarket accommodation on the airport road. The rooms are luxurious affairs, complete with daybeds, balconies and silks. There's huge bathtubs, nice big TVs, a/c and a good choice of eating options including a decent café. Khmer-owned and themed add to the attraction.

$$$$ Apsara Angkor Hotel, Route 6 (between the airport and town), T063-964999, www.apsaraangkor.com. Pretty standard hotel for the money they are asking. Well-appointed rooms with all amenities but they are rather kitsch. Facilities include gym, internet, swimming pool. Visa/MC/AMEX.

$$$$ Empress Angkor, Airport Rd, opposite cultural village, T063-963999, www.empress angkor.com. One of the newest luxury hotels in town. The wooden interior is much nicer than you'd expect from the outside. 207 cosy guestrooms with all the usual inclusions, plus cable TV and balcony. Hotel facilities include restaurant (international and local cuisine), bar, massage, gym, swimming pool, jacuzzi spa and sauna. Visa/AMEX/MasterCard/JCB.

$$ Jasmine Lodge, Airport Rd near to town centre, T012-784980, www.jasmine lodge.com. One of the best budget deals in town Jasmine is often fully booked, and with good reason. The super-friendly owner Kunn and his family go out of their way to make this a superlative place to stay – there's free internet and Wi-Fi, breakfast can be included in the rate upon request, huge shared areas for sitting, book exchange, tour bookings, bus tickets, etc. There is a huge spread of rooms from basic fan rooms with shared facilities all the way up to sparkling new accommodation with a/c, TV and hot water bathrooms. Highly recommended.

$$ Paul Dubrule Hotel and Tourism School, airport road about 3 km from town centre, T063-963672, www.ecolepaul dubrule.org. Set up by its namesake and founder of the **Accor** hotel group, the Paul Dubrule school has to be one of the best bargains in town. Sure, you'll be looked after by wide-eyed trainees and there's only a skeleton staff after 1800, but the rooms, themed on the local hotels that help sponsor the project, are excellent value. There are only 4 to choose from, the most expensive representing the best deal. All are a/c, with TV, hot water and including breakfast. Recommended.

$ Bou Savy, just outside town centre just off the main airport road, T063-964967, www.bousavyguesthouse.com. One of the best budget options in town this tiny and very friendly family-owned guesthouse is set in soothing gardens and offers a range of rooms with fan or a/c. They also offer breakfast, cheap internet and have some nice public areas. Recommended.

$ Earthwalkers, just off the Airport Rd, T012-967901, mail@earthwalkers.no. Popular European-run budget guesthouse. Good gardens and pool table. Bit far out of town.

Kompong Thom and around *p57*
$$$ Sambor Village, Brocheatebatey or Democrat St, 10-min walk from junction with road No 6, T062-961391, www.sambor village.com. Kompong Thom's most upmarket place is not a bad effort. The pleasant tiled rooms come with 4-poster beds, private terraces, hot water bathrooms, a/c, free Wi-Fi and cable TV. There's a small pool set in a nice garden and free bicycles for guests. Breakfast is also included.

$$ Stung Sen Royal Hotel, T062-961228. Friendly place with good-sized a/c rooms in a quiet location overlooking the river. For the price things are a little basic but still a good option.

$ Mittapheap Hotel, on NH6 just before you cross the bridge into the town centre, T062-961213. The usually clean though musty rooms set in this Khmer villa come with a/c, hot water and TV. It's sited by the river and one of the rooms also has a balcony.

$ Arunreas Hotel, on the corner, beside the market, on NH6, T062-961294. The accommodation is quite out of place in the town with lifts, Las Vegas-style lights and bell-hops. Rooms are clean with a/c, hot water and cable TV. Make sure you get a room towards the top of the hotel as the karaoke can be absolutely heinous, particularly if you are tired from a day exploring the temples. Cheaper rooms can be had with fans at the sister guesthouse next door, **Arunreas Guesthouse**.

T'Beng Meanchey and around *p58*
Accommodation here is pretty basic.
$ Phnom Meas, opposite the taxi stand, T012-632017. Small, clean rooms with fan, attached bathroom and TV. The friendly staff have opted to paint the rooms a nauseating shade of green.

$ Prum Tep Guesthouse, on the main road about 2 km from the Vishnu traffic circle T012-964645. Clean, hospital-like rooms with a/c, fan and bathroom. Recommended.

$ 27 May Guesthouse, on the main road beside the market, T011-905472. Concrete building with pokey rooms with fan or a/c.

Angkor Wat *p29*

Outside the entrance to Angkor Wat is a large selection of cafés and restaurants, including the sister restaurant to the **Blue Pumpkin** in Siem Reap, serving good sandwiches and breakfasts, ideal for takeaway. Near the pond there are a number of cheap food and drink stalls, bookshops and posse of hawkers selling film, souvenirs, etc.

Chez Sophéa, outside Angkor Wat, T012-858003 is a unique place in the evening serving Khmer and French cuisine. Romantic setting. Closes around 2100, but later if you want to stay for a digestif.

Anlong Veng *p51*

Rumour has it that between here and T'beng Meanchey lots of chickens used for cooking have died of starvation (which one could guess from looking at the mere carcasses). And it is also advisable to avoid fish as some (but not all) have probably been caught at Ta Mok's Lake, believed to contain human remains at some point in time (not particularly threatening these days but still unpleasant).

The small town shuts down relatively early so try to get in for dinner before 1900. At all restaurants most meals will be under US$4.

Chom No Tror Cheak, across from Ta Mok's Lake. Has the best variety of food in town. Mixed Thai and Khmer food. English menu.

Darareaksmei Restaurant, on the main road near the roundabout, T011-559171. Whether you like this restaurant or not might depend on how you rate Khmer singing as it doubles as a local entertainment venue (provided by a synthesizer and local talent). In this case, whoever invented karaoke has a lot to answer for. The music aside, this is one of the better restaurants in town with an English menu and Thai and Khmer food. Soup, quail, *lok lok*. A bit pricier than other places but that covers your entertainment for the night!

Lapia, on the main road as you enter town. This little restaurant offers soup-style meals on individual cookers placed at each table. There is no English menu but with a few instructions the children that run the restaurant can prepare something tasty. The noodles are fantastic.

Restaurant 168, overlooking Ta Mot's Lake, T092-225544. Very popular Khmer restaurant right on the shore of the lake. Individual fairy huts have been built so diners can eat in privacy and enjoy the view. Good local food available at reasonable prices.

Siem Reap *p53, maps p54 and p63*

Thanks to the growth in mainly foreign-owned restaurants there is now an excellent selection of eating places. Thai, Indian and Asian are particularly well represented but a good number of French and other European restaurants also now compete for the traveller's dollar. Siem Reap is markedly more expensive than Phnom Penh (often double the price). The Old Market area has, over the last few years, become the main area to eat and drink, though the choice of hotels in this area is severely lacking.

Town centre

Barrio, Sivatha St, away from the central area. T012-756448. 1000-late. Fantastic French and Khmer food. A favourite of the expats. Recommended.

FCC, Pokamber Av, T063-760280. Sister to the Phnom Penh restaurant, this one is a bit more schmick. Good range of world-class food and drinks, nice surroundings, great armchairs, sophisticated.

Le Malraux, Sivatha Bvld, T063-966041, www.le-malraux-siem-reap.com. Daily 0700-2400. Sophisticated French cuisine served in this excellent restaurant. Also do some Khmer and Asian dishes, great wine list and good cognacs. Patio or indoor seating. Recommended.

ṬṬṬ L'Oasi Italiana, long way up East River Rd, T092-418917. 1100-1400 and 1800-2200 (closed Mon lunchtimes). Attractive leafy location with high-quality Italian menu.

ṬṬṬ-ṬṬ Sala Bai Restaurant School, Taphul Rd, T089-590864, booking@salabai.com. Taking in students from impoverished backgrounds from the poorest areas of Cambodia, **Sala Bai** trains students in hotel and restaurant skills and places them in establishments around town. Service is not the best as students are quite shy practising their English, but a little bit of patience will help them through. Open for breakfast and lunch only. Highly recommended.

ṬṬṬ-ṬṬ Soria Moria Fusion Kitchen, Wat Bo Rd, T063-964768. 0700-2200, serves a range of local, Scandinavian and Japanese specialties. Wed nights is the popular US$1 night where all tapas dishes and drinks including cocktails cost US$1 each.

ṬṬ Bopha, on the east side of the river, slightly up from Passagio, T063-964928. Fantastic Thai-Khmer restaurant in lovely, tranquil garden setting. One of the absolute best in town. Recommended.

ṬṬ Butterflies Gardens, just off Wat Bo Rd, T063-761211, www.butterfliesofangkor.com. Daily 0800-2200. Tropical butterflies flit around a koi-filled pond in this slightly odd eatery. The food is Khmer/Asian and is average but the setting is well worth a visit.

ṬṬ Le Tigre de Papier, Bar St, T012-659770. Best pizzas in town and offer Khmer cooking classes with profits benefiting a local hotel training school.

ṬṬ The Sugar Palm, Taphul Rd, T012-818143. Closed Sun. Sophisticated Khmer restaurant, immaculate service with casual ambience.

ṬṬ Viroth's Restaraunt, No 246 Wat Bo St, T012-826346. 1100-1400 and 1900-late. Upmarket place offering very good modern Khmer cuisine plus a few Western staples. Looks more expensive than it actually is and is good value.

Ṭ Curry Walla, Sivatha St and next door to the noon till night market, T063-965451. Best Indian cuisine in town at very good prices. 2 locations in town, no difference in style or menu, ambiance varies. Recommended.

Ṭ Khmer Kitchen, opposite Old market and Alley West, T063-964154. Tasty cheap Khmer dishes service can be a little slow, but the food is worth waiting for. Sit on the alley side for good people watching. Recommend their pumpkin pies (more of an omelette than a pie!).

Ṭ Moloppor Café, east of the river, near **Bopha Hotel**. Good cheap Japanese and pizzas.

Around the Old Market (Psar Chars)

There are some cheap market-stall type restaurants around the Old Market and further up Sivatha St, near the Central Market, across from Sokimex petrol station.

ṬṬ The Blue Pumpkin, Old Market area, T063-963574. Western and Asian food and drinks. Sandwiches, ice cream, pitta, salads and pasta. Candidate for 'least likely eatery to find in Siem Reap' with its white minimalist decor. Good breakfasts and cheap cocktails. Eat on the 2nd level. So popular they can be seen at various locations around town and across from Angkor. Recommended if you need a retreat for half an hour.

ṬṬ Dead Fish Tower, Sivatha Blvd, T012-630377. 0700-late. Thai and Khmer restaurant in a fantastically eclectic modern Thai setting. Multiple platforms, quirky decorations, sculptures, apsara dance shows, small putting green and a crocodile farm all add to the atmosphere of this popular restaurant.

ṬṬ Molly Malone's, T063-963533. Lovely Irish bar and restaurant offering classic dishes like Irish lamb stew, shepherd's pie, roasts and fish and chips.

ṬṬ The Red Piano, northwest of the Old Market, T063-963240. An institution in Siem Reap, based in a 100-year-old colonial building. Coffee, sandwiches, salad and pastas. Cocktail bar, offering a range of tipples, including one dedicated to Angelina Jolie (who frequented the establishment while working on Tomb Raider).

Singing Tree, Alley West, Old market area, T012-2589846, www.singingtreecafe.com. 0730-2100. Serves tasty European and Khmer home cooking, with plenty of veggie options and great fruit shakes.

Soup Dragon, T063-964933. Serves a variety of Khmer and Vietnamese dishes but its specialty is soups in earthenware pots cooked at the table. Breezy and clean, a light and colourful location sitting on a corner terrace surrounded by plants. Upstairs bar, happy hour 1600-1930.

Tell, 374 Sivatha St, T063-963289. Swiss, German, Austrian restaurant and bar. Branch of the long established Phnom Penh restaurant. Serves excellent fondue and raclette, imported beer and sausages. Reasonable prices and generous portions.

Airport Road

There's now a seemingly endless run of Asian restaurants on this road. Some are quite good though you may struggle to find a menu in English.

Abacus, off airport road behind Aceleda bank, T012-644286, wwwcafeabacus.com. Open daily 1100-late. A little further out from the main Old Market area, this place is considered one of the best restaurants in town. Offering French and Cambodian, everything is fantastic here. The fish is superb, the steak is to die for. Highly recommended.

Paul Dubrule Hotel and Tourism School, airport road about 3 km from town centre, T063-963672, www.ecolepauldubrule.org. As well as being a great place to stay, the school also offers a pretty good set lunch. It can be hit and miss but the quality is often very high and they are always eager to keep their guests happy. Your money will also go to support an excellent vehicle for development – some of the school's graduates have gone

on to be well-paid chefs at some of Asia's top hotels and restaurants.

Kompong Thom *p57*

Stung Sen Royal Restaurant, attached to the hotel of the same name. The best pick for food in town. It is set up for tour groups with white linen and silver service. It feels a bit weird going in there to eat when you are the only diners (with 4 people waiting on you). Excellent Khmer food and some Western dishes (omelettes, etc). Good value

Arunreas Restaurant. Despite smelling like a wet dog this place serves reasonably cheap, quick Chinese and Khmer food from a large menu. Okay service but the waitresses are usually run off their feet dealing with locals.

Lay Kim Seng Restaurant, behind the market. Also doubles as a bus stop so turns out food very quickly. Large, cheap menu with Asian staples, noodles, rice, soups, etc. There is often a hawker selling pretty good steamed pork rolls outside.

T'Beng Meanchey *p58*

There isn't a huge selection of restaurants in T'Beng Meanchey but the few there are offer Khmer food at very cheap prices (a meal and drinks under US$4). There is a row of Khmer restaurants all offering pretty much the same fare in town, on the road towards the Naga Traffic Circle.

Chan Reas Restaurant, a block south of the Acleda Bank. Friendly restaurant with palatable Khmer food.

Dara Reah Restaurant, on the corner, near the Vishnu roundabout. Despite the unfortunate name, this is probably the best place to eat in town, with an English menu and good selection of Khmer food. Its forte is dinner. Recommended.

Market Restaurant, on the right-hand side of the market. This place is hugely popular with the locals who like to have a cuppa and tune into the wrestling. Worth a visit if only for the bizarre sight of watching what seems like the entire male population of the town 'ooohh' and 'ahhh' over the wrestling. Its coffee is much better than its food.

¶ Mlop Dong Restaurant, opposite the taxi stand. Cute little restaurant offering good coffee, omelettes and noodles alongside other Cambodian fare. Good option for breakfast.

♪ Bars and clubs

Siem Reap *p53, maps p54 and p63*
Angkor What?, on street known as 'Bar Street', Old Market Area, T012-490755. Open early evening to early morning. Bar run by friendly staff, popular with travellers and young expats.
Fresh at Chilli Si Dang, East River Rd, T017-875129, 0800-late. Laid-back atmosphere, friendly service away from the tourist drag. Happy hour between 1700 and 2100.
Laundry, near the Old Market, turn right off 'Bar St', T012-246912. Open till late. Funky little bar.
Linga, Laneway behind 'Bar St', T012-246912. Gay-friendly bar offering a wide selection of cocktails. Great whiskey sours.
Miss Wong, The Lane (behind Pub St) T092-428332. 1700-0100. Cute little bar serving sharp cocktails in an Old Shanghai setting.
The Red Piano, Old Market Area, T063-963240. A comfortable bar/diner furnished with large wicker armchairs. The good international menu is fairly priced. Happy hour 1600-2100.
Temple Bar, on 'Bar St', T015-999909. Popular drinking hole, dimly lit, good music. Not related to its seedier counterpart in Phnom Penh.
The Warehouse, opposite Old Market Area, T063-964600. 1000-0300. Popular bar, good service and Wi-Fi.
X Rooftop Bar, Top of Sivataha St (you'll see the aluminous X from most high-rise buildings in town), T092-207842. 1600-sunrise. The latest closing bar in town.

Happy hour between 1600-1730.
Zone One, Taphul Village, T012-912347. 1800- late. Place to go to experience local nightlife.

⊛ Entertainment

Siem Reap *p53, maps p54 and p63*
Dance performance
A number of hotels, notably **Le Grand**, **Sofitel** and **Angkor Village**, stage Khmer dancing performances in the evening. There are a few dance shows performed by local children from orphanages; be aware that sometimes these kids are dancing every night to tourists. They may look cute but one might consider whether they should be working late 7 days a week.

Cambodian Cultural Village, on the airport road, 6 km from town. Tickets US$12.

Music concerts
A popular Sat evening attraction is the one man concert put on by Dr Beat Richner (Beatocello), founder of the Jayavarman VII hospital for children. Run entirely on voluntary donations the 3 hospitals in the foundation need US$9 million per year in order to treat Cambodian children free of charge. He performs at the hospital, on the road to Angkor, just north of the **Sofitel** hotel, at 1915 every Sat, lasts about 1 hr, free admission but donations gratefully accepted. A worthwhile experience.

Shadow puppetry
Shadow puppetry is one of the finest performing arts of the region and is an absolute must for visitors to the area.
Bayon Restaurant, Wat Bo St. Has regular shadow puppet shows in the evening.
Krousar Thmey, a local NGO, often tours its shadow puppet show to Siem Reap. The show is performed by underprivileged children (who have also made the puppets) at **La Noria Restaurant** on East River Rd. Wed at 1930 but check as they can be a tad

irregular. Highly recommended. Donations accepted.

○ Shopping

Anlong Veng *p51*
With 2 shiny new shopping plazas complete with fast food, escalators and a/c and Alley West smartening up with cheeky chic boutiques, Siem Reap is fast improving its reputation of being more than just a temple stopover. Anything and everything can be obtained from the bustling markets (a relatively new addition to a town that was forbidden to trade in anything too Western or modern during the Khmer Rouge days).

Siem Reap *p53, maps p54 and p63*
Art
Happy Cambodia, Old Market area. Sells the works of French Canadian Stéphane 'Stef' Delaprée. Colourful, cheerful images of everyday Khmer sights and scenes. Originals up to US$385, good-quality prints US$25-40, cards and t-shirts.

Books
Street booksellers (usually people with disabilities) are in abundance, selling copied versions of the old favourites.
Blue Apsara, near the Old Market, carries the best variety of used books in town.

Clothes
Rogue, Old Market area, T012-703264. Sells a range of easy-to-wear casual clothing.
Wanderlust, Alley West, T012-529924. Colourful clothing with ethical flair. The American fashion designer has strong fair trade principals.
Wild Poppy, Sivatha St, T077-568874. Classic comfortable clothing, locally made.

Handicrafts
Chantiers Écoles, down a short lane off Sivatha St, T063-963330. School for orphaned children which trains them in carving, sewing and weaving. Products are on sale and raise 30% of the school's running costs. Outlets selling the school's products are dotted around town under the name **Les Artisans d'Angkor**. There is a silk production centre 15 km out of town, T063-380369, open daily 0730-1730.
Senteurs d'Angkor, opposite Old Market, T063-964860. Sells a good selection of handicrafts, carvings, silverware, silks, handmade paper, cards, scented oils, incense, pepper and spices.

Markets
Outside Phnom Penh, Siem Reap is about the only place whose markets are worth browsing in for genuinely interesting souvenirs. Old Market (Psar Chars) is not a large market but stall holders and keepers of the surrounding shops have developed quite a good understanding of what tickles the appetite of foreigners. All manner of Buddhist statues and icons are on sale. Reproductions of Angkor figures are also available in various degrees of craftsmanship. There is a selection of silk and cotton fabrics, kramas and sarongs, nice silverware, books, CDs and DVDs. Leather puppets and rice paper rubbings of Angkor bas-reliefs are unusual mementos.

In the night market area, off Sivatha St, you will find bars, spas and cafés. The original night market, towards the back, has more original stalls, but is slightly more expensive.

Supermarket
Angkor Market, Sivatha St, T063-767799. Everything you need or miss can be found here, even marmite.
ATC – Angkor Trade Center, Pokambor Av behind the Old Market area. Well stocked convenient shopping on way back from town to Wat Bo area.
Star Mart, the supermarket attached to Caltex petrol stations, is very well stocked. Open 24 hrs.

▲ Activities and tours

Siem Reap *p53, maps p54 and p63*
Therapies
Khmer, Thai, reflexology and Japanese
massage are readily available. Many
masseuses will come to your hotel.
Frangipani, Hup Guan St near Angkor
Hospital for Children, T063-964391,
www.frangipani siemreap. Aromatherapy,
reflexology and other professional
treatments.
Mutita Spa, at Borei Angkor Resort and Spa
on Route 6, T63-964406. Offers unique J'Pong
thearpy a traditional Cambodian heat and
relaxation treatment using herbal steam.
Seeing Hands. Massage by seeing impaired
individuals. US$3 per hr. Highly
recommended.

Tour operators
Many hotels and guesthouses can organize
and recommend tour guides and services on
arrival.
Asia Pacific Travel, No 100 Route 6,
T063-760862, www.angkortravelcambodia.
com. Also has offices in Vietnam and Laos.
Exotissimo Travel, No 300 Airport Rd,
T063-964323, or head office (Phnom Penh),
T023-218948, www.exotissimo.com. Tours of
Angkor and sites beyond.
Hidden Cambodia Adventure Tours,
Trang Village, House No 1, Slokram
Commune, T012-655201, www.hidden
cambodia.com. Specializing in dirt bike tours
to remote areas and off the track temple
locations. Recommended for adventurers. For
example: to Koh Ker, 4 hrs.
Journeys Within, on the outskirts of Siem
Reap towards the temples, T063-966463,
www.journeys-within.com. Specializes in
private, customized tours that allow visitors to
enjoy the temples as well as go further afield
to see the everyday lives of Cambodians.
PTM Tours, No 552, Group 6, Mondul 1,
T063-964388, www.ptm-travel.com.

Reasonably-priced package tours to Angkor
and around Phnom Penh. Also offers cheap
hotel reservations.
Terre Cambodge, on Huap Guan St near
Angkor Hospital for Children, T092476682,
www.terrecambodge.com. Offers tours with a
twist, including cruises on an old sampan boat.
Not cheap but worth it for the experience.
Two Dragons Guesthouse (see page 65)
can also organize some off-the-beaten-track
tours. The owner Gordon Sharpless is a very
knowledgeable and helpful fellow.
World Express Travel, St No 11 (Old Market
area), T063-963600. Can organize tours all
over Cambodia. Also books local and
international air/bus tickets. Good place to
extend visa. Friendly service.
WHL Cambodia, Wat Bo Rd, T063-963854,
www.angkorhotels.org. Local website
booking hotels and tours with a responsible
tourism approach.

⊖ Transport

Anlong Veng *p51*
From Anlong to **Siem Reap**, **T'beng
Meanchey** or **Kompong Thom**, one must
endure enormously potholed roads and
broken bridges. Shared taxis/pickups leave in
the morning for **Siem Reap**, US$3-4, 3-4 hrs.
The road between Anlong Veng and **Preah
Vihear** (90 km) is comparatively smooth for
this region (in the dry season) and pickups
leave from the market around 0700, US$2.

Siem Reap *p53, maps p54 and p63*
Air
The airport (REP), T063-963148, is 7 km from
Siem Reap. There are flights from **Phnom
Penh**, **Ho Chi Minh City**, **Hanoi**, **Bangkok**,
Singapore, **Kuala Lumpur**, **Pakse** and
Vientiane. The airport has a taxi service, café,
internet access, phone service and gift shop.
A moto into town is US$1, taxi US$7.
Guesthouse owners often offer free rides.
There is US$25 departure tax at Siem Reap
airport.

Airlines Bangkok Airways, Airport Rd, www.bangkokair.com, 6 flights a day to **Bangkok**. Jetstar Asia, www.jetstarasia.com, flies to **Singapore** 3 times a week. Malaysian budget airlines **Airasia**, T023-890035, www.airasia.com, to **Kuala Lumpur**, daily flights. **Helicopters Cambodia**, 658 St Hup Quan, near Old Market, T063-963316. New Zealand company offering chartered flights around the temples. **Lao Airlines**, T/F063-963283, Mon-Fri 0800-1700, Sat 0800-1200. To **Vientiane**, 3 flights a week via **Pakse**. **Malaysia Airlines**, T063-964135, 3 times a week to **Kuala Lumpur**. Vietnam Airlines, Airport Rd, T063-964488, www.vietnamairlines.com. To **Ho Chi Minh City**. Silkair, T063-426808, www.silkair.com, daily flights to **Singapore**.

Boat

Boat to and from **Phnom Penh**, US$35, 5-6 hrs. The trip is fantastically atmospheric and a good way to kill 2 birds with 1 stone and see the mighty Tonlé Sap Lake. The boat is a less appealing option in the dry season when low water levels necessitate transfers to small, shallow draft vessels. In case of extremely low water levels a bus or pickup will need to be taken for part of the trip. The mudbank causeway between the lake and the outskirts of Siem Reap is hard to negotiate and may necessitate some walking (it is 12 km from Bindonville harbour to Siem Reap). Boats depart from the Phnom Penh Port on Sisowath Quay (end of 106 St) 0700, departing Siem Reap 0700 from Chong Khneas on the Tonlé Sap Lake. Tickets and enquiries T012-581358.

To **Battambang** the fast boat takes 4 hrs, US$25. Note that there are frequent mechanical breakdowns and in the past occasional reports of boats being shot at by irate fishermen whose nets have been snagged.

Bus/pick-up/shared taxi

The a/c buses are one of the most convenient and comfortable ways to go to and from **Phnom Penh**, US$6-11, 6 hrs. Almost every guesthouse or hotel sells the tickets although it is easy enough to pick up from the bus stations/terminal. Companies include **GST**, **Mekong Express** and **Capitol**. Most buses depart between 0630-0800 near the Old Market. The best service is the Mekong Express, US$11 if you buy in advance. It has the quickest service, 5 hrs and a/c with a little bit of info over the mike.

In peak periods, particularly Khmer New Year, it is important to purchase tickets a day or 2 prior to travel. A shared taxi to Phnom Penh will cost you US$10, minimum 4.

To **Battambang**, most guesthouses can organize a ticket for US$10, 7 hrs.

To **Anlong Veng**, roughly 3-4 hrs via NH67 on the way to Banteay Srei. Shared taxis/pickups leave from the market daily but not regularly, US$103-104. Siem Reap motodops will usually quote the price at US$30 a day for the trip but one should be discerning as you need a bike and driver who will be able to cope with the harsh roads. **Hidden Cambodia**, does tours with both dirt bike and 4WDs of the area (**Anlong Veng**, **Preah Vihear**, **Preah Khan**, etc) for around US$100-130 per day.

Car and bicycle

Most hotels and guesthouses rent cars with drivers and US$2 per day for bicycles. **The White Bicycles** scheme has been set up by ex-pat Norwegian NGO workers as a way to provide not only a source of income and work for locals but also to develop a charitable fund that supports children and teenagers in Cambodia. The bikes cost US$2 a day to rent with US$1.50 going to the charitable fund and US$0.50 going to sustain and repair the bikes by employing and training locals. The White Bicycles can be found at several hotels and guesthouses

throughout Siem Reap,
www.thewhitebicycles.org.

Kompong Thom *p57*

Kompong Thom is 146 km from Siem Reap and 162 km from Phnom Penh. To the north, T'Beng Meanchey is 151 km of mainly rough road with the turn-off to Preah Khan about 90 km from Kompong Thom. The taxi/bus station is just a block east of the main road in the centre of town. Shared taxis depart all morning for **Siem Reap**, US$6, **Phnom Penh**, 3 hrs, US$5, and the occasional one to **T'Beng Meanchey**, US$6-8. **GST Bus Company** runs 3 buses a day between **Phnom Penh** (from the Central Market) and Kompong Thom (from Pich Chenda Restaurant). The bus departs from both places at 0645, 0745, 1200, US$5. **Phnom Penh Public Transport Buses** depart from the Central Market at 0645, 0730, 1215, US$3.

T'Beng Meanchey *p58*

Almost every way you approach T'Beng Meanchey is tough. T'Beng Meanchey is 151 km north of Kompong Thom and the road is not in great shape. The trip will take at least 4 hrs in the dry season and considerably more during the rains. A shared taxi to **Kompong Thom** is US$6-8 If you want to visit Koh Ker or Preah Khan from here there are numerous motos at the taxi stand who will take you. Expect to pay between US$10-20 per day. Even if you have your own motorbike it's worthwhile hiring one of the motos to guide you as the tracks can by labyrinthal.

❶ Directory

Anlong Veng *p51*

Banks Acelda, turn right at the only roundabout on the main road, bank is just after Lucky Hotel, T092-466546. **Telephone** If you wish to make a phone call some of the local 'phone-boxes' (ie someone with a mobile) will let you make calls within Cambodia for 600 riel per min.

Siem Reap *p53, maps p54 and p63*

Banks ATMs can be found all over town. **ANZ Royal**, Old Market and Tep Vong St, T06-3969700. Efficient friendly service. **Cambodia Commercial Bank**, 130 Sivatha St, 0900-1600. Open Sat and Sun. Currency and TC exchange. Advance on Visa, MasterCard, JCB, AMEX. **Canadia Bank**, Old Market Area, T063-964808, Mon-Fri 0800-1500. Moneygram, MasterCard advances, currency and TC exchange. **Krong Thai Bank**, 10-11 Sivatha Blvd. Mon-Fri 0800-1500, Sat 0800-1200. Currency exchange, TCs. **Mekong Bank**, 43 Sivatha St, T063-964417, Mon-Fri 0830-1600, Sat 0830-1200. US dollars TCs cashed, 2% commission, cash advance on Visa and JCB cards only. Western Union services. **Union Commercial Bank**, north of Old Market, Mon-Fri 0800-1530, Sat 0800-1200. Cash advance on MasterCard and Visa, cashes TCs and has an ATM. **Internet** Rates vary but should be around 3000-4000 riel per hr. Most internet places now offer internet calls. Most bars, restaurants, cafés and guesthouses have complimentary Wi-Fi for those utilizing their services. **Medical services** Medical facilities are okay here and improving but by no means of an international standard. In most cases it is probably best to fly to Bangkok. **Royal International Hospital**, Airport Rd, T063-39911. Good standard and costs can be claimed back from most international insurance companies. **Children's hospitals**: **Jayavarman VII Hospital**, on the road to Angkor Wat. **Angkor Hospital for Children**, Achamean St. Provincial hospital north of Old Market. Pharmacies: opposite the entrance of the provincial hospital. **Post office** On Pokamber Av, west side of Siem Reap River, but it can take up to a month for mail to be delivered. 0700-1700. **DHL**, Sivatha St (opposite petrol station), will send urgent letters for US$50, guaranteed 4-day delivery. **Telephone** Sim cards are readily available to purchase with a passport in most phone shops for US$10-25 and will let you call overseas.

Kompong Thom *p57*
Banks **Acleda Bank**, NH6, before the bridge, does Western Union transfers (no credit card advances). There are a number of money changers in front of the market.
Internet There are 2 internet shops on NH6 before the bridge, on the right-hand side of the road and a couple of other places around the market. Internet is quite expensive and ranges from US$2-4 per min. **Post office** There is quite a good post office, a block from the market, which can deliver

international mail. **Telephone** There are a number of local 'phone-boxes' (people who will rent you their mobile phone) sprinkled around town, particularly in the market area. Overseas calls can be made at most internet shops for around 800 riel per min.

T'Beng Meanchay *p58*
Communications There isn't a whole lot of access here – the post office is nothing more than a 2-way radio and mobile phones don't have great coverage. **Buddhist for Development** has set up an internet café where you can make international calls for around 1000 riel per min; internet, US$2 per hr.

Contents

Footnotes

Useful Khmer words and phrases

There are a number of sounds in Khmer, or Cambodian, which have no equivalent in English. The transcription given here is only an approximation of the sound in Khmer and is taken from David Smyth and Tran Kien's (1991) *Courtesy and Survival in Cambodia*, School of Oriental and African Studies: London.

Consonants

bp	is a sharp 'p' somewhere between 'p' and 'b' in English	g	as in 'get'
ch	as in 'chase'	kh	a 'k' as in 'kettle'
dt	is a sharp 't', somewhere between 't' and 'd'	ng	as in 'ring'
j	as in 'jump'	ph	a 'p' sound as in 'pill', not an 'f' sound as in 'phone'

Vowels

a	as in 'ago'	i	as in 'fin'
ah	as in 'car'	o	as in 'long'
ai	as in 'Thai'	oh	as in 'loan'
ao	as in 'Lao'	oo	as in 'boot'
ay	as in 'pay'	OO	more of a 'u' sound as in 'cook'
ee	as in 'see'	u	as in 'run'
eu	as in 'uugh'		

Useful words and phrases

yes	*baht (male speakers)*	good afternoon	*tiveah suor sdei*
	Jah (female speakers)	good evening	*sa-yoanh suor sdei*
		good night	*reah-trey suor sdei*
no	*(ot) dtay*	excuse me/sorry!...	*...som dta(h)*
please	*suom mehta*	where's the...?	*...noev ai nah?*
thank you (very much)		how much is...?	*...t'lai bpon-mahn?*
	or-gOOn (j'run)	it doesn't matter	*mun ay dtay*
hello	*jOOm ree-up soo-a*	never mind/that's alright	
goodbye	*lee-a hai*		*dop bprum moo-ay*
see you later	*juab k'nea ta'ngay krai*	I don't understand	*mun yoo-ul dtay*
		I want a...	*k'nyom jang baan*
how are you?	*Tau neak sok sapbay jea teh?*	what is your name?	*Neak ch'muah ei?*
		my name is...	*k'nyom tch much*
good morning	*arun suor sdei*		

Basic vocabulary

bank	*ta-nee-a-gee-a*	market	*p'sah*
doctor	*bpairt*	post office	*brai-sa-nee-ya-than*
hospital	*mOOn-dti-bpairt*	toilet	*borng-goo-un*
Khmer Rouge	*k-mai gra-horm*	water	*dteuk*

Food

bread	*nOOm bpung*	meat	*saich*
chicken	*moan*	restaurant	*hanng bai*
delicious	*ch'ngun*	rice	*bai*
fish	*dt'ray*	tea	*dtai*
food	*m'hohp*	water	*dteuk*

Travel

is it far?	*Ch'ngai dtay?*	Monday	*t'ngai jan*
turn left/right	*bot dtoh kahng*	Tuesday	*t'ngai ong-gee-a*
	ch'wayng/s'dum	Wednesday	*t'ngai bpoot*
go straight	*ondtoh dtrong*	Thursday	*t'ngai bpra-hoa-a*
where is the...?	*noev eah nah?*	Friday	*t'ngai sok*
bus	*laan ch'nuol*	Saturday	*t'ngai sao*
boat	*dtook*	month	*khaeh*
train station	*ra dteah plerng*	year	*ch'nam*
cyclo	*see kloa*	next year	*ch'nam groy*
will you go for...riel?...	*ree-ul bahn dtay?*	January	*ma ga raa*
that's expensive	*t'lai na(h)*	February	*kompheak*
		March	*mee nah*

Time/date

morning	*bpreuk*	April	*meh sah*
midday	*dtrong*	May	*oo sa phea*
night	*yOOp*	June	*mi thok nah*
today	*t'ngai ni(h)*	July	*ka kada*
day	*t'ngai*	August	*say haa*
tomorrow	*sa-aik*	September	*kan'ya*
yesterday	*m'seri mern*	October	*dto laa*
midnight	*aa-tree-at*	November	*wech a gaa*
Sunday	*t'ngai aa-dteut*	December	*t'noo*

Numbers

1	*moo-ay*	20	*m'pay*
2	*bpee*	30	*sahm seup*
3	*bay*	40	*sai seup*
4	*boo-un*	50	*hah seup*
5	*bprum*	60	*hok seup*
6	*bprum moo-ay*	70	*jert seup*
7	*bprum bpee or*	80	*bpait seup*
	bprum bpeul	90	*gao seup*
8	*bprum bay*	100	*moo-ay roy*
9	*bprum boo-un*	1000	*moo-ay bpohn*
10	*dop*	10,000	*moo-ay meun*
11	*dop moo-ay*	100,000	*moo-ay sain*
12	*dop bpee... etc*	1,000,000	*moo-ay lee-un*
16	*dop bprum moo-ay*	10,000,000	*dahp lee-un*

Index